EMAILS FROM THE E

Lynn Santer: http://www.lynnsanter.com

Foreword

After years of having been dubbed "The Email Queen" (a name given to me by one of my closest friends, Alfred Hitchcock's iconic star of "The Birds", Tippi Hedren) and hundreds of requests to publish some of my funnier emails I finally conceded when one particular email received more rave reviews than any book I'd ever written! The email in question concerned an encounter with bureaucracy that would have driven a saint to homicidal tendencies and to kick off this book I will commence with that particular email. However the emails encompass a wide variety of topics from the antics of my faithful pooch through to life-changing circumstances. Most, I hope, will have you crying with laughter, but a few here and there might make you stop and think.

Of course before any of this could happen I first had to collect and collate emails from across the years, most of which I hadn't retained. Thinking it was completely futile I sent, you guessed it, a few emails off to those who had been recipients of some of these gems. Quite a few people came through with a dozen or so that they'd retained, which was surprising enough to me as I was amazed they'd even been read, never mind kept for posterity, but the biggest shock of all came from one man who had kept every single email I'd sent him for **seventeen years**! And when you learn who that man is you might find it even more surprising.

In 1994 I had written a screenplay (my first) with a devil character in it. I thought Jack Nicholson would be perfect for the role (of course I did). So how do I go about getting Jack? Somehow (I don't even remember) I procured the name and phone number of his agent – Sandy. Somehow I bluffed my way into a meeting with him. >>>

I still don't know, and really must ask him one day, why he agreed to the meeting because the screenplay was the most woeful and amateurish you can imagine… although the concept was quite brilliant (if I say so myself). Off I flew to Hollywood.

Back then Sandy's office was in Encino. When you've been Jack Nicholson's agent since 1961 you have nothing to prove to anyone. I dressed my best (of course I did) was nervous as an Arab at a Bar Mitzvah (this was my first meeting in Hollywood ever… what a way to start) and headed out to his office. It was very small, modest, and plain, in fact there was nothing to read in the waiting room whatsoever – not a magazine, newspaper – nothing.

Twiddling my thumbs nervously and looking around I saw what looked like a weather-beaten old bible on the receptionist's counter. I picked it up and read the title "All I know about Show Biz by Sandy xxxxxx". Well, I thought, that's got to be worth a read. I opened the cover only to discover to my dismay and astonishment that the whole book was written in Japanese! "You bleep, bleep, bleep," I thought to myself. "I like you!" (I admire chutzpah!)

Anyway, we met. He was dressed in very casual attire and there were no photos of Jack in the office, just Sandy's dogs. We started talking about animals, and somehow we connected on that level. He politely declined my screenplay but the meeting was pleasant and friendly enough and that was that.

Six months later I was flying through LA again, from Australia to somewhere. I saw some didgeridoos in the airport for sale, some small enough to fit in my suitcase (this is the traditional musical instrument of the Australian Aborigines). By their side was a pile of instruction books on how to play it in all languages… including Japanese. Guess which one I bought (of course I did!) >>>

Sandy just thought this was the funniest thing ever – it turns out that he admires chutzpah just as much as I do. A friendship sprung up from that point which has seen us in weekly communication from that day to this (and even a few meals here and there as I flitted through LA from time to time). However, not in a million years would I have imagined he would have kept every email I ever sent him, and I mean the one liners, the requests to sign petitions, the notifications of e-cards sent – everything. I can't begin to imagine what the storage capacity on his computer must be like! It's true… size does matter!!!

Perhaps in poetic justice Sandy attempted to send all these emails to me as one file – it was 70 MB – my computer went kablewie!!!! But God Bless Sandy – he then went to the effort of sending them all to me ten at a time! That took… a while (several days).

THANK YOU SANDY!!!

And thank you too to my good friends Guy Thomas and Shane Greaves, who also went hunting for old emails to include in this book, but **a particularly special thank you to Anita Herrick, the PA of my dear friend Tippi Hedren, who had to go digging into archived HARD COPY FOLDERS to find physical print outs of some of the older hilarious emails from adventures on my sister's farm and others involving the wildlife on the lake where I live. Anita I am truly humbled and deeply grateful that these emails warranted saving and you went to such great effort for me!**

THANK YOU ANITA!!!!!!!

I hope the rest of the world enjoys them as much as you apparently did.

From: Anita Herrick
Sent: Friday, 15 April 2011 8:19 AM
To: 'Lynn Santer'
Subject: RE: Just found this

Here are the last of them.

In the past few months I have tossed out a lot of stuff –
however, I always considered some of your emails works
of art!!!!! I could not toss them!!!

Enjoy – I am so very pleased I could help you!!!

Lots of hugs,
Anita

CONTENTS

The email that started it all

So… after four years with my Magical Scarecrows books and DVDs on Amazon, Amazon suddenly decided to write to me and asked me to complete a W-8BEN form for the IRS. Why, I hear you ask? Because Amazon need this on file for when they are audited to show they are not withholding the statutory 30% tax from my Royalties because under Article 12 of the treaty between Australia and the US this is not required. I tried to explain I don't earn any Royalties as I have only made the books and DVDs available through this service because it is the cheapest, most professional, and efficient way to procure the products on demand for when I gift them to charities and needy children around the world. They are only listed on Amazon because it's all part of the same service that makes them so easily available to ME. If I make a sale a year it's a lot. Amazon is a commercial organisation – this did not compute.

"We have to have your W-8BEN so we don't have to withhold 30% tax – think of all the tax you'll get back."

"Excuse me, you are not listening to me, I won't get any tax back because I don't earn any Royalties – the only person who buys the books and DVDs is me."

"But you'll get all your tax back."

"HELLO!!! Am I speaking Swahili? What tax?"

"It is a requirement that you complete a W-8BEN."

"Okay, I surrender, fine, I'll complete the dang form – send it to me."

You think it's that simple? Oh no fear!!!! First, so Amazon advised me, I have to obtain an EIN. >>>

What's an EIN, I hear you ask? It's an Employee Identification Number, and they very kindly sent me the link on the IRS website to complete the form.

Compliantly, dutifully, and obediently (can anyone imagine me being any of those things?) I clicked the link and started to complete the form. I didn't get very far before it asked me for my SSN. What's an SSN, I hear you ask? It's an American Social Security Number. Funnily enough I don't have one of those.

I tried to explain this to Amazon. It did not compute.

I decided I would get more sense out of the IRS (which will tell you roughly how desperate I was!!!) so I called them – ON THE PHONE – in the US. I spoke to a very congenial, helpful, and crushingly sincere polite person at the other end (who sounded all too over the whole day to be bothered with anything) and attempted to explain the situation. At this point I was told I couldn't apply for an EIN (no kidding – I'd already worked that one out for myself) but I could apply for an ITIN. What's an ITIN, I hear you ask? That's an Individual Tax Identification Number. Okay, I'll have three of those please. No, seriously, one will do thank you. Amazon said I could do this exercise on line, is that right? Of course it wasn't right!!! This form needs to be downloaded, printed, completed, and submitted by snail mail, and then it will take THREE MONTHS to turn around. But do you think that's all? No fear!!!

To submit a W7 form to receive an ITIN one must accompany it with a letter from Amazon stating why the aforementioned ITIN is required, and a copy of my passport, notarised by an AMERICAN notary. I wrote back to Amazon.

>>>>>>>>>>>>>>>>>>>>>>>>>>>>>>>>>>>

Dear Amazon… putting aside my pending nervous breakdown, the IRS tell me that I can apply for an ITIN which will suffice for your W-8BEN provided I get a letter from you stating why the aforementioned ITIN is required and a copy of my passport authorised by a notorious American person. We don't have any notorious Americans in Australia, or perhaps we do but I don't know any of them personally (okay, I didn't actually say that last part). Amazon wrote back…

It is against our policy to give you a letter.

EXCUSE ME? WHAT? YOU WANT THIS FRICKING FORM – IT'S FOR YOUR BENEFIT, NOT MINE, AND IT IS AN IRS REQUIREMENT THAT ***YOU*** PROVIDE A LETTER SO I CAN OBTAIN ONE.

The automaton response reaffirmed that writing a letter was against their policy, but short of being actually helpful they would do anything they could to help.

My nervous breakdown now in full swing, I called – ON THE PHONE – in the US - the IRS again… and waited on hold for 45 minutes. When I finally heard "Hello" the battery in my handset went dead!!!!!!!!! I'm not making any of this up you know!!!!!!! Fortuitously my fax machine has a handset. I pounced on it with all the ravening desperation of a starving predator. "Hello? IRS? Are you still there?" They were. Phew!!! I explained the situation – again…

The IRS could not believe that Amazon would not issue a letter and asked, "Do you have their email requesting the W-8BEN?" Yes I did. "Do you have their email stating they will not issue a letter?" Yes I did. Was this good? Were we making progress, I wondered hopelessly against hope? The very congenial, helpful and crushingly sincere polite person on the end of the phone suggested that >>>

I submit those with my W7 form requesting an ITIN and my own covering letter and who knows… it might work… it would only take THREE MONTHS to find out, but you never know, luck could be with you (luck or the force…whatever)… which leads me to another point. I explained to very nice congenial, helpful crushingly sincere polite person in the IRS that I did not know any notorious Americans (that would be NOTARIES) in Australia, would an Australian one suffice? They said they would have to check that, would I mind holding while they refer to the treaty between Australia and the US? Sure, why not? I'd only been on the phone to America for nearly an hour, to receive a tax return, of… oh yes… NOTHING… sure, go ahead and check the treaty… why not, after all I have nothing whatsoever better to do with my time (or my sanity!!!).

Yes, the treaty says notorious Australians are acceptable. I almost felt like popping champagne. You think that's all? No fear!!! At this point the lovely IRS person came up with an idea. Why not submit a 1040NR. Well, why the heck not I thought. Sounds like fun to me. At this point I'm just about blubbing my lips with my finger tip in knife edge insanity so what the heck did I care what number form I submitted to whom??? Sure, I'll do that. What is it? Can I have three?

A 1040NR is a Non Resident return claiming withheld tax back. DO WE ALL REMEMBER THERE ISN'T ANY TAX AT THIS POINT? But hey, I'm up for it if it gets my ITIN. How does that work? Well go to xyz and then abc and then download the form. I did that. What's the first thing I see? PLEASE ENTER YOUR TAX IDENTIFICATION NUMBER HERE!!!!!! Excuse me while I just wash this bottle of valium down with a vat of vodka. "No, no, no," the congenial, helpful crushingly sincere polite person urged me. "DON'T PANIC! All you need to write in there is NUMBER PENDING" >>>

(why couldn't I do that in first place?) But anyway... I was advised to submit this form because then I would automatically be issued with an ITIN, all I needed to do was submit it with my notorious AUSTRALIAN signature on my passport copy and my 1042S from Amazon.
EXCUSE ME? MY WHAT?..............

The 1042S is the form Amazon should send me stating my Royalties earned and tax withheld so I can claim the tax back on the 1040NR (are you following this???). The only problem is, because I don't earn Royalties and therefore they don't withhold tax, I hadn't received a 1042S. "You haven't received a 1042S?" the IRS person gasped. "How can that be?" I attempted to explain that this led to that which went to the other... that lived in the house that Jack built and the nice men in white suits would be turning up any second now to take me away to talk to the trees!!!!!!!!!!!!!!

I then wrote back to Amazon and explained ALL of this, adding, with sobs in invisible ink between the lines, "I'm only doing this to help underprivileged children – it's true what they say, isn't it – no good deed ever goes unpunished – I'm now in floods of tears and I hope you're satisfied!!!"

They were not. But they did promise to issue me with a 1042S (which I am still waiting for) and once again assured me that doing anything short of actually being helpful they would do anything they could to help.

Now if you think that's hilarious…

Getta load of this…

From: xxxxx, xxxxx [mailto:xxxxxxx@amazon.com]
Sent: Thursday, 14 April 2011 8:31 AM
To: Lynn Santer
Subject: RE: Create Space account

Hi Lynn,

Please mail your W-8BEN to the following address when you are ready:

8329 West Sunset Road
Suite 200
Las Vegas, NV 89113

Please let us know what happens with your application. Because of your case, I am hoping we will soon be able to issue an ITIN letter to all members. I know that probably does not make you feel any better, but should your application fail because of this, please do let us know. By that time, we may be in a better position to help you with this issue.

Kind Regards (name deleted)

Hey, if my actions, correspondence and that email (yes I did actually send it to Amazon as well!!!!) manage to change the policy of a goliath like Amazon and make the world a little easier for future authors, then my work here is done!!!!

And when I told Amazon what I was doing...

From: xxxxx, xxxxx [mailto:xxxxxxx@amazon.com]
Sent: Thursday, 14 April 2011 10:33 AM
To: Lynn Santer
Subject: RE: Create Space account

Hi Lynn,

I think that cover and the book idea are fantastic. Your emails are truly animated and enjoyable to read.

I love your foreword and wish you all the best of luck with this new book!

I am sure we will correspond again soon.

Kind Regards,

(Name deleted)

Antics of

CHELSEA...

The "Sub-Woofer"

From: Lynn Santer
Sent: Tuesday, January 11, 2011 11:50 AM
To: Tippi Hedren

I really love my dog, but grrrrrrr…..

Chelsea decided it was just absolutely imperative she went out for a pee yesterday afternoon (inclement weather not withstanding) so…

I grabbed a large golf umbrella and took her out the back – well, she's an old lady dog and there's no reason she needs to get rheumatic/arthritic joints just because our weather is ghastly. So…

She found a burning need to investigate every single blade of grass to find precisely the right spot (of course she did – grrrrrrrrr) leading me straight down to the end where there was washing drying on the line (did I say "drying"???) Who the hell puts washing out in this weather???) The golf umbrella became completely entangled in one of mom's bras (of course it did – grrrrrrrrrrrr) while Miss Chelsea continued undaunted to investigate each individual blade of grass… now with sodden fur (naturally) and… guess what……………… decided not to pee after all!!!!!!!!!!!!!!!
She skipped back inside, extremely happy with herself, while I was still attempting to untangle the golf umbrella from mother's bra (too many word pictures???) – oh - and by the way – I was drowned by that point too (grrrrrrrrrrrrrr) and when I finally returned inside she was very happily rolling herself all over my Versace bedspread to get dry (GRRRRRRRRRRRRRRRR) as I approached her with a big towel and she LEAPT off the bed and into the lounge – onto mother's lap, quivering "Protect me – protect me – mad, crazy, umbrella tangling mommy with very big scary bath towel" and then absolutely REVELLED in the rub down!!!!!!!!!!
Hummmmmmmmmmmmmmmmmmmmmmmm……………

From: Lynn Santer
Sent: Monday, September 06, 2010 4:09 PM
To: 'Anita Herrick/Tippi Hedren'
Subject: Chelsea – **What a brave and cute dog!!!**

A drama with Chelsea, but she came through it with flying colours!! She was operated on between 11.30 and 12.30 yesterday. We picked her up at 2.30 and were told she might be a bit drowsy for a while – she was bouncing off walls and leaping on furniture, racing around the house, barking at cats, wagging her tail – it was quite astonishing! She's incredible! What a star!!!!!! Mom and I were basket cases, of course, because we'd always been told a general anaesthetic could spell the end for Chelsea because of her heart condition, and she was under for quite a time while the operation took place. The poor dog had TWO teeth that were completely rotted to the core – she must have felt terrible but never once gave any indication of it. If I hadn't noticed her face was swollen the other night we never would have known at all, and ultimately the poison would have killed her. Now, as I type, she been up, been out, had something to eat, and decided to go back to bed – my bed (of course) and all you can see is two little ears poking out from under the sheets. She looks so cute I took a picture, then she looked up, so I took another picture, and then she went, "Na – too early" and threw her head back down. Adorable – see here…..

Spot the dog

From: Lynn Santer

Whatever power it is - it picks its moment!!!!

Date: Tue, 20 Oct 2009 15:05:32 +1000

Jeepers…

I just went to Bernie's Pet Barn to buy Chelsea some of her favourite treats, and on the way back everything just fell in on top of me. Not only what you know about (Alain suddenly dying, walking into Chelsea's warm vomit barefoot in the middle of the night when she was ill recently, the disaster event at Versace, e-bay not believing my T-shirt is real [!#!@#!^#!^!(^!(%&!##!}, Priscilla finally saying no to that big project) and now poor Chelsea seems destined to have to manage on three legs as a result of rupturing her cruciate ligament this weekend as she can't be operated on due to her heart condition, but add to ALL that that my sister Karen called last night and she's undergoing a barrage of medical tests for we know not what, and sitting at home watching trashy DVDs because she feels so awful… all alone… all the way up in Darwin… and Karen NEVER takes a sick day.

On the way home from Bernie's it just all became too much and I started balling my eyes out while I was driving!!!! Not exactly something I'm prone to doing!!!! I didn't know what to do. I seriously considered swinging by the Synagogue to cry all over there, but then my mobile rang………..

I thought, "I don't care who this is, I'm going to cry all over whoever it is. It could be Kirstine from A Current Affair, it could be Jenny from New Idea – I DON'T CARE!!!!"

I answered the phone feeling all sorry for myself, and (crikey!!!) it was Lincoln Lewis's agent!! >>>

You may recall the gorgeous Barry Crocker became so insistent about Lincoln being the right person to play Alby in our film (especially as Lincoln will be older and with several major credits under his belt by the time we come to film anything) that Paul eventually sanctioned a query call. The call was met with almost orgasmic enthusiasm (some weeks ago) but first the agent had to like the book, and second Lincoln had to like the project................

And then.............

Mike Lake, who is former head of production at Village Roadshow, now based in Hollywood, and an old friend of Paul Mason (the Alby film producer) is pretty keen to be the money man/exec producer on the film, and he's coming to the Gold Coast in a few weeks.

Of course I had to get my act together PDQ. I still had tears streaming down my face and was in desperate need of a tissue (which I didn't have one of anywhere) and had to sound all chipper and professional – and worse still answer pointed questions... which I did... of course.

May I say............. OY VEY......... And Chelsea's very happy with her treats.........................

From: Lynn Santer
Subject: RE: Stop the world!!!!
Date: Mon, 24 May 2010 16:42:26 +1000

It never rains but it pours!

Crikey!!! If I was washing down valium with vodka before the big event at the Million Paws Walk (with bushfires to put out every day leading up to the event, including the morning of the day with Emily Williams losing her voice for crying out loud… she had to mime!!!!!)……..

First – I had mom in emergency straight after Ria (Alby's sister) returned to South Australia on Monday.

Next – we discovered Chelsea had fleas… pooping in my bed no less (MAJOR YUKKY YUKKY POOS BARS!!!!)

Then – mom was admitted to hospital on Tuesday – in for a week – out of hospital on Saturday – out two days – then back into hospital THIS morning with BP @ 198/105 (and I am supposed to be finalising a book THIS week and starting on Mr McDonald's book NEXT week).

But wait – there's more!!!!!!!

Chelsea hasn't been able to keep any solid food down since yesterday. When she even threw up the tiniest crumb of boiled chicken – back down to the vet. The poor dog had her temperature taken (you put that thing WHERE?) and a stingy injection, and… AND… I cannot give her ANYTHING to eat for 24 HOURS!!!!!! She's going to think I hate her!!!!!!! I've been given a food supplement to mix in two litres of water. Do you think I could find ANYTHING to measure two litres of water in??? Don't be daft!!!! That was $100 (consult, injection and mixy stuff). If she's still throwing up tomorrow it's >>>

blood tests ($160) and if its pancreatitis then it's overnight at the vet's on fluids (don't even want to think what that'll cost).

Meanwhile we pray its only gastro, and definitely pray it's not a liver or kidney issue. At her age it could be any of the above. If she's okay after 24 hours then it's boiled chicken and rice... no "choccie bars" (roo sticks) so she's REALLY going to think I hate her – the poor love.

STOP THE WORLD – I WANT TO GET OFF!!!!!!!!

Just spoke with mom this moment. Needless to say I didn't tell her any of this. Her specialist won't be in until 8pm tonight!!! She has headaches and is bored out of her brain. She was so happy to be home and now no one knows know what to think.

Where's that valium and vodka????

Oh yeah... and the new pool lining is staining with dropped leaves that aren't scooped out in 24 hours!!!!!!!!

I just had to turn off, even for five minutes, so I ran a big bubble bath in the spa, poured a chilled glass of chardonnay, turned off the lights, and took in my portable CD player with some soothing meditation music on it. Ah... bliss... until... I popped the headphones on, turned around to pick up a bar of soap, and pulled the CD player into the tub with me!!!!! It FRIED!!!!!! And if it had been plugged into the mains (rather than battery operated) so would I have!!!

All I can say is OY VEY!!!!!!! **AND IF YOU THINK I'VE STAYED OFF CIGARETTES THROUGH THAT LOT... YOU'RE TRIPPIN'!!!!!!!!!!!!!!!!!!!**

Too funny not to include

The Andre Rieu Concert

Date: Thu, 4 Dec 2008 09:12:51

The concert was amazing. Anyone who hadn't seen it before, and didn't know what was coming, would have absolutely had their socks knocked off. Le Mommy is thrilled to her tippy toes that she's been, she's seen, and knows for certain the man who motivated her to learn how to use the Hi Fi is actually real – and that makes everything all worth while, but............................... I just have to share with you some back story...........................

First of all I worked so hard trying to make up for what I knew would be an effective week's loss of productivity I came down with the mother of all cold viruses just two days out from DefCon 1 status. Assuring my quack that the world *would* in fact stop spinning and life as we know it *would* end if I was unable to accompany Le Mommy on this jolly jaunt that has been her reason for getting out of bed every day for the last year, I was duly doped up. Feeling like death would be welcome I bravely applied the war paint as full DefCon 1 readiness approached and we headed off in the direction of Queensland's answer to Sin City, Bris Vegas.

Once nestled into almost adequate accommodations, selected by Le Mommy solely based on their proximity to le venue of le Andre's stage spectacular, I quickly dosed up on some extra drugs and, after a brief but meaningful executive meeting with myself, decided washing them down with a fine cognac would be a rather splendid idea. Having arrived a day early, as Le Mommy was fearful of being late (!!!!!) this permitted me a little down time to rest and recover with a dose of my own obsession... no, not cognac but Stargate (whose DVDs I had thought to bring with me). >>>

I actually slept quite well on night one (dunno how that happened) and hence felt relatively refreshed to have breakfast with the manager of Suncorp Stadium yesterday morning; a perfectly charming man whom I no doubt infected with my dreaded lurgy.

Perhaps as a result of breakfasting with Le Mommy, perhaps not, Suncorp broadcast a warning shortly after breakfast…. Truly!!! The warning was to advise patrons of Le Andre's "anything you can do I can do bigger" event to get to the stadium as early as possible (starting after breakfast was advised… almost) as for the first time in the stadium's history the place was going to be filled with a 26,000 strong audience mainly comprised of clueless geriatrics (no disrespect intended) who were unfamiliar with this fine establishment of hallowed ground purpose built for the holy of holies – Australian Rugby. Quietly I think the authorities were actually concerned and wanting adequate time to monitor the blue rinse groupies for the possible illegal trading of illicit denture glue, or perhaps a bit of prosthetic limb swapping **(NO DISRESPECT INTENDED).**

I have to say on approach to the stadium I did swallow a wry smile as, due to Le Mommy's connectedness to Le Stadium Manager we were travelling the five (or so) meters to Le Stadium from Le Almost Adequate Accommodations in a less than luxurious vehicle BUT one of only two that had an ACCESS ALL AREAS pass, SOOOOOOO…. We were permitted access through all road blocks when irate limos and even a Rolls Royce were turned away and told to enter with the rest of the great unwashed **(NO DISRESPECT INTENDED).**

We were appropriately ushered into the only cushioned seats in Le Stadium, in the VIP section (again thanks to Le Mommy's connectedness to Le Manager) and we sat… and we waited… all nerves a tingly twit of >>>

ant.........ic...........ip..............ation............ AND
THEN...................................

LOUD SPEAKER ANNOUNCEMENT: Ladies and
Gentlemen

[Audience holds collective breath thinking their beloved
Andre is about to appear – for real – in the flesh – all
prayers finally answered.]

LOUD SPEAKER ANNOUNCEMENT (CONT'D):
Ladies and Gentlemen, may I have your attention please.
You may have noticed the weather has taken a turn for the
worse.

[Audience gasps and groans... a few pace makers gave
out.] (No disrespect intended.)

LOUD SPEAKER ANNOUNCEMENT (CONT'D): Radar
telemetry (did the clueless geriatrics know what radar
telemetry was, I asked myself).... Radar telemetry shows
that a grade (whatever it was) storm is rapidly approaching
the stadium so for your comfort and safety would you all
please move into the concourse.

[Audience remains seated like stunned mullets]

LOUD SPEAKER ANNOUNCEMENT (CONT'D):
I MEAN ***NOW***
(Okay, he didn't use those words, but did use that
sentiment.)

There was a brief flurry as trade was finalized on the illicit
denture glue and prosthetic limbs were swapped back for
storm escaping at maximum velocity, and... we're off...
slow... slow... quick... quick... CHARGE >>>

Once gathered in one of two places: (a) a sweat box the Japanese concentration camps would have been proud of, or (b) a death-trap tunnel of "stampede-in-the-making" (if only all the prosthetic limbs had been swapped back correctly) those near the opening watched as Mother Nature put on a more spectacular display than Le Andre ever could have… oh boy… what an absolute cracker of a storm!!!! My only consolation (being unreasonably furious at this point, and still feeling like death would be welcome from the virus I was harbouring) was the knowledge that in the hot and humid conditions with suitable whisking breezes I was certainly effectively spreading my green lurgy infection (that I was courageously masking… God Bless Christian Dior and the pharmaceutical industry) swiftly across the 26,000 "Andre Tragics" surrounding me in every direction… i.e. those gnashing their newly glued dentures in dismay wondering if they would ever get to see their beloved Andre.

(I know this all sounds terribly rude, but please take it as humour… it is <u>NOT</u> a serious commentary!!!)

At one point, gathered in what must have been reminiscent of a WWII bomb bunker, word filtered through from those nearest the entrance that an announcement had been made advising the storm would pass in 20 minutes. I turned to pass on the intell to Le Mommy. Trying not to look too hopeful Le Mommy replied, "I'm not saying anything." The words were NOT out of her mouth when she'd turned to the Andre Tragic, Blue Rinse, Denture Glue Gnashing, Clueless Geriatric behind her to spread the glad tidings of comfort and joy because the Messiah in fact could soon appear. That is Le Mommy's idea of not saying anything!!!!!!!! Not one second later a thunder clap directly over the stadium almost shook the foundations of this extremely solid building and knocked a few >>>

hearing aids right out of their ear sockets. Twenty minutes my..... grandmother! Never one to have my spirits dampened (I may consume them but shall never surrender to sunken psyches) I did the only thing a self-respecting writer could do... I whipped out pen and paper and began jotting this journal as peering four-eyed spectators looked curiously on.

It has to be said I could not commend more highly the expert, and unflappable, staff at Suncorp Stadium who could not have handled the situation more expertly and superbly... they could have been trained at Disneyland. Brilliant, brilliant, utterly brilliant. And furthermore they were seamlessly pleasant without a tone of officiousness or exasperation in their management of the confused and disappointed masses. Superb.

One hour later.......

Cheers erupted as the announcement spread like wildlife, or at least a snail on steroids, that the rain had passed and we could return to our seats. Everyone was issued with paper towels to dry the plastic chairs so our delicate little tushies weren't too moist to enjoy the show, nor to leave us with unpleasant mementos that would be unmentionable. Rather than waiting to make his usual entrance, Andre and his orchestra were immediately on stage as the dash of walkers, wheelchairs and walking sticks hobbled at Olympic speed back to their assigned viewing positions, his first words being...
"They told me it never rained in Brisbane!"
(No, but boy does it pour!)
He then played – and you have to love him for this – SINGING IN THE RAIN as everyone returned in a civilized fashion to the auditorium.

Following that more than appreciated rendition, the Messiah's next announcement was that the Minister >>>

was present and had granted special dispensation for the show to continue past the normally permitted curfew to enable the entire show to be performed… just proving the man really does walk on water. Then again with an entourage of 550 cast and crew, 100 containers of props and staging, $6.5 mill per state to produce, etc… THE SHOW MUST GO ON!!!

Midway through a further announcement was made… ALL public transport would run later than normal for free to allow everyone to get home. Incredible. With a big thank you to the Minister, Andre informed everyone there was no reason to leave early and every last note could be savoured.

The highlights of the show were without doubt the flying angel, which was simply stunning, and the Aussie girl has a voice truly direct from heaven, and the Australian pipers who marched in after the show was supposedly officially over during the encore to perform Amazing Grace, which always takes my breath away. Both the entrance and the performance was enormously impressive.

I have to hand it to him… the man knows how to put on a show.

Now… back to the salt mines.

Good things always ☺ xxxxxx
Lynn Santer

My mates write funny emails too!!!

From: Mike Pilcher
Sent: Wednesday, 10 March 2010 11:31 AM
To: Lynn Santer
Subject: Om

Lynn

Of course. Sorry I didn't reply. I was busy.

Nick and I had gone out to the Gaucho restaurant on Westbourne Grove and put paid to a cow, a sheep and a small pig. Very tasty. Unfortunately Nick was feeling a little under the weather and went home early. A great night out with a pal finished a bit early and so I went home. I was writing an email and was listening to Radiohead. An acceptable end to a good night out...................

Tuesday 10.39 pm I decided I wanted the desert we decided we didn't need in the restaurant.

Tuesday 10:40 pm I determined to go out to the local store and get said desert. I could taste it already.

Tuesday 10:41 pm I am in the lift in my apartment building. It is a small space. It's a long lift journey so I start to wonder. Hmm. I have seen those films of people chimney climbing rock formations. Hmm. I wonder if I reach out with my legs. Yes. I can put my back against one wall and reach my leg to the other. First one. Then two. Within seconds I am all of 4 ft off the lift bottom and 44 ft off the ground. I am Ranulph Finnes. The conqueror of all things urban and lift. After 10 seconds, sweat, swearing, and a groin strain, I realize I cannot get 4ft 1inch from the base of the lift. I try again. No joy. Augh. So I drop. I am apparently heavy. Is the lift telling me I am fat? I am not fat. It stops anyway. >>>

Tuesday 10:42pm The lift is more immobile and intransigent than a lawyer. It's OK. I can be persuasive. So I kick it. The sign says, "Lift out of service." No. That can't be right. "How much service do you want? 15%?" Nope. Damn thing is not responding to kicks or bribes. OK. I will work smooth charm. I press the buttons. Nope. "Lift out of service." In little annoying red pixels that look like they should be advertising something in a 1980's shop window, like "Really good haircuts only 5 quid." Or "Great kebabs - chicken and lamb." or "No sticky seats" No I am not in Amsterdam and no kebabs and no haircuts. Just, "Lift out of service." No problem. I press the button that says, "Alarm". Cool. A whizzy, high-pitched noise. Now they're listening. I will be out in a trice. Half a trice.

Tuesday 10:44pm Somebody in Mumbai answers. OK. No problem. HSBC outsources there, it will all be OK. I calmly explain I am stuck in a lift. Yes I am on my own (why does that matter?) In Notting Hill. No not Motting Bill. On Westbourne Grove. No not Westbirne Road. My name is Mike. No I am not on a bike. I tell myself it will all be OK. I ask the simple question, "When will the engineer get here?" No clue. OK, five minutes or five hours? Apparently time is relative and relative to me it is not relevant. No problem. I will wait. I thank them very much for their kind attention. For I am Zen.

Tuesday 10:46pm Still Zen. Om.

Tuesday 10:47pm OK. Not Zen. Where the hell is the engineer? This is a very small lift. Is there enough air in here? I start to calculate my lung capacity and the size of the lift. I calculate I have at least 14 hours of air. So why is it so stuffy? Zen. Om. You lived in California for ten years. Om.

Tuesday 10:48pm Screw Om. This is Notting Hill. >>>

Where is the damn engineer.? I start to calculate the time it would take to get from Mumbai to West London. I don't much like those numbers. I think I need to pee. Not actually sure I do, but in the event I do. What does one do? Search for a urinal. No urinal in the lift. Hmm. The sign says, "Lift out of service." No directions to a urinal. Om.

Tuesday 10:51pm I am 40 feet in the air. Hmm. I am fine. I am not in a lift. I am in fact on my way to get dessert. Om. OK. I don't even make a minute of this crap. I am in a lift and I don't want to be here. I want to get out.

Tuesday 10:52pm I try to CTRL/ALT/DEL the lift. It appears that no combination of the buttons causes anything other than mild cramp in my fingers. It's just software for Christ's sake. Is this software revenge? Did I sell too much stuff that didn't work? Is karmic balance righting itself? I didn't write the stuff. Om.

Tuesday 10:54pm I remember all those films where people escape from tight spaces. In this case there is no escape hatch. Despite pushing on every surface there is no hidden escape. Om. Om?

Tuesday 10:55pm I decide to actually be Zen. I have seen the Shawshank Redemption. You can be locked in a small space for decades. OK that's boring. I try to tunnel my way out. I get my house keys and start scratching at the imaginary poster of Rita Hayworth. Damn I hate stainless steel. No wonder Sheffield was replaced by Shanghai. Sheffield steel was too good. If this lift was made in China and I lick the walls do I get lead poisoning? Om.

Tuesday 10:57pm I am now angry. Hell what did I do? I tried to scale a lift. So the hell what. Damn the lift. Damn stainless steel. Damn dessert.

Tuesday 10:58pm OK Om. I am better than this. What >>>

did Steve McQueen do when locked in solitary? I have no tennis ball. Damn. I decide to count the spots on the floor of the lift.

Tuesday 10:59pm There are 436 spots. Now what?

Tuesday 11.00pm Calling Mumbai. I calmly I explain again I am stuck in a lift. Yes I am on my own (why does that still matter?) In Notting Hill. No not Motting Bill. On Westbourne Grove. No not Westbe Road. My name is Mike. No I am not on a hike. I tell myself it will all be OK. I ask the simple question, "When will they engineer get here?" No clue. OK, ten minutes or ten hours? You don't know? No problem. I will wait.

Tuesday 11.01pm OK tired of waiting I call Mumbai again. I talk to Simon (who I suspect is actually called Summeet). I enquire if I give them four hundred pounds, how long will it take? Still no idea. Om.

Tuesday 11.02pm I decide to ignore the sticky grey plastic floor and sink to it and sit quietly rocking back and forth. Om. I decide this is all my fault. I did not speak nicely enough to the waiter tonight, or I ignored a needy purveyor of the Big Issue. It is all my fault. I am stuck in a lift. I have a sticky bad smelling plastic grey thing stuck to my ass, I am 40 ft in the air and it is my fault. I am sorry. I decide my penance shall be to sit quietly until help comes and I am liberated like the French in 1944. I sit quietly. I set the stop watch on my Swiss time piece to make certain I do not trouble the kind people in Mumbai. It is not their fault. It is mine. I tried to chimney climb a lift. I am humble. I sit and meditate. If I am here for the next four days, it is my recompense. All will be good. I look at my watch. 11 hours have gone by. My bladder does not hurt. I am not hungry. I can share this advanced state of mind with all I meet. For I am Zen. >>>

Tuesday 11.04pm Upon deeper analyzing apparently less than 2 minutes have passed. No that cannot be right. The little bitty hand on my sports watch tells me it is only 1 minute and 55 seconds since I was last Zen.

Tuesday 11.05 and 55 seconds pm I call Mumbai. We have the whole, when is the lift dude getting here conversation and I follow with. "Let's assume there's a fire in the building and I am stuck in the lift. Now what happens?" "Is there a fire?" "Assume there is Sunjeet, now what?" The squawky noise in the lift through the strange speakerphone went quiet. I think Sunjeet's brain has melted. Muzak ensures.

Tuesday 11.15pm I am in fact now really Zen. All is good. I am in a green field and the world smells of posies.

Tuesday 11.25pm Om.

Tuesday 11.26pm Noises. I hear a buzzer go. At last. I am saved. I will live. There is air, there is water. Now one buzzer. Answer the door you donkey. Another. Are they all asleep? Soon every buzzer in the building is ringing.

Tuesday 11.27pm a knock on the door. Expecting an East European ex-Stasi employee to be working the lift on a Tuesday night I open the door.

Tuesday 11.28pm I think I may be embarrassed. There are four big blokes in fireman uniforms at the door of the lift. I assume this is to make me feel better and the lift company knows how to relax distressed customers. Nope. They are fireman. Apparently there was a fire. In the lift. Somebody told them. At least they let me out before Sainsbury's closed.

PS. for what it's worth the fireman's benevolent fund is now significantly better off than at 10.39pm.

You just can't make this stuff up

Tiger Woods plays with own balls, Nike says

ON TEENAGERS, ADULT:

Statistics show that teen pregnancy drops off significantly after age 25.

Mary Anne Tebedo, Republican state senator from Colorado Springs (contributed by Harry F. Puncec)

MONDAY   DECEMBER 1999

QUESTION OF THE DAY

Question: What constitutes a millionaire?

Answer: A millionaire is someone who has $1 million, according to Jerry Beto, branch manager and senior vice president of investments at AG Edwards and Sons.

Do you have a question of general interest? We'll answer one question of broad community interest in the paper each day. E-mail your question

---

JAY CRONLEY

One-armed man applauds the kindness of strangers

The other afternoon, a man and a woman came to my door.

Army vehicle disappears

AN Australian Army vehicle worth $74,000 has gone missing after being painted with camouflage.

Police are seeking public help to find the four-wheel drive, which was

Fish need water,

Feds say

By Phil Hayworth

While conservation groups and others wel-

County to pay $250,000 to advertise lack of funds

BY MATT COOPER
The Register-Guard

Lane County will spend up to $250,000 this year publicizing its tight financial picture, in hopes that voters in November will approve higher taxes for public-safety services.

It's an amount for county spending on publicity that has been unparalleled in at least the past 10 years. And it illustrates the seriousness of the effort to persuade voters

Utah Poison Control Center reminds everyone not to take poison

"Children Act Fast, So Do Poisons" is the theme for National Poison Prevention Week, arch 20 - 26. The Utah Poison Control Center (UPCC) would like to take the opportunity to remind parents and caregivers that poisonings can be prevented. In 2004, the Utah Poison Control Center responded to over 50,000 calls, the majority of which were about actual potential poisonings.

Over 60 percent of the potential poisoning exposures involved children under age 6. The top five substances that children in this

giving or taking medicine. Check the dosage each use.
* Avoid taking medicine in front of children.
* Never refer to medicine as candy.
* Clean your medicine cabinet periodically, safely disposing of unneeded and outdated medicines.

The UPCC, part of the College of Pharmacy, has an active community outreach program. In 2004, representatives of the Utah Poison Control Center provided 126 community presentations and distributed more than 40,000 poison prevention education materi-

Federal Agents Raid Gun Shop, Find Weapons

Store Owner Arrested Previously

By Brian Barber
World Staff Writer

Federal agents on Monday searched a south Tulsa gun shop owned by the man who officials allege had kept in his [...]

On July 2, undercover narcotics agents served a warrant at Thao's home, [...] to search for drugs. They found a stockpile of land mines, hand grenades, dynamite and other explo-

with driving after suspension and driving an unregistered vehicle following a traffic stop on Maple Street.

2:58 p.m. — The Learning Center on Hanson Street reports a man across the way stands at his window for hours watching the center, making parents nervous. Police ID the subject as a cardboard cutout of Arnold Schwarzenegger.

3:18 p.m. — A kitten on Shaw Drive apparently has "rectum

Medford police Monday.

Miscellaneous

■ **Dog attack** — Lower Duck Pond, Lithia Park, Ashland. Police responded to a report of two dogs running loose and attacking ducks at about 11:20 a.m. Sunday.

The officer cited a resident for the loose dogs. The duck refused medical treatment and left the area, according to police records.

■ **Jail releases** — Jackson

Police checked the area and found an open door in the back of the building. An officer went inside and called out, "Marco."

The man's name was not Marco, detective Tim Dohr said. Instead, "the officer was trying to inject some humor into the situation."

Police found the suspect after he responded, "Polo."

The restaurant manager

And one for all of us to remember…

about the new store locating on
Lower Third Street.

nop

ily

n he

dria

llaı

ikes

mily

Debra Jackson said she likes
shopping at the Dollar Palace
because it is convenient and
casual.

"I don't have to get all dressed
up like I'm going to Wal-Mart
or something," she said, adding
she shops at Williams' store "to

Ireland 's worst air disaster occurred early
this morning when a small *two-seater*
Cessna plane crashed into a cemetery. Irish
search and rescue workers have recovered
2826 bodies so far and expect that number to
climb as digging continues into the night.

Auntie Lynn strikes again

Re: Magical Scarecrows Reading and Event – The Great Synagogue in Sydney (to my sister...)

The newly appointed "second unit Rabbi" (assistant Rabbi) turned out to have gone to the same schools as I did in London – we even had the same teachers – both primary and secondary. Amazing!

Things were a little chaotic as the apparently hand-picked, invitation-only (not community wide) guests poured in, and I was concerned at first how attentive they may be, but once I started my presentation every single child, and even all the adults, were spellbound. Big cheese Rabbi, my mate Rabbi Lawrence, arrived late (!!) so I threw him a cheeky salute across the room as he walked in. Everyone turned around and he threw me a cheeky salute back with a big grin – very cute. There were many raised eyebrows in the congregations – tee hee.

After the kiddie session there was a break while children were ushered into a separate area for activities before the adult session on how to encourage your child in creative writing began. During this time a woman I didn't know (who turned out to be big cheese Rabbi's mom) came up to me and said of my kiddie story reading presentation, "My dear that was just absolutely enchanting." Very cool.

Then it was time for the grown up session and once again I was frankly staggered at how completely I held everyone's attention – especially when I learned one of them was a producer with "Australian Story"!! The feedback afterwards was heart-warming – and gushing – although I wasn't entirely sure big cheese Rabbi had been paying full attention as he seemed to have been texting a lot, but >>>

when he showed me his phone he had in fact been taking detailed notes of everything I'd said!!! Howzat??

It had started to rain before we were due to leave so big cheese Rabbi told his mom and me he would go and bring the car around – how gallant – a chauffeur Rabbi – excellent!

We went to the finest kosher restaurant in Sydney for dinner where big cheese Rabbi ordered a drink for himself that had apparently recently been taken off the kosher list. The restaurant owner was highly amused that big cheese didn't know and had asked for it, to which I naturally quipped, "Bad Rabbi" and he jokingly hit himself over the wrist – too funny!!! Over dinner I learned that big cheese's mom volunteers at a refuge for battered Jewish wives. After I finished choking at the shock that such a place even existed (!!) I quickly discovered that wasn't the biggest shock. There are also Muslim refuges for battered Muslim wives, but battered Muslim wives won't go to them – they come to the Jewish one! Why? Two reasons: (a) they know that kosher food is also hallel, and (b) they know that Jews won't summarily send them back to their husbands!! How about them apples??!!

Discussing some of the cases understandably made my blood boil, but I said it was best not to say what I was thinking I would do to the abusers in front of a Rabbi!!!

Big cheese told me the reason I had kept the children quiet and captivated (against all odds) was because they were not used to anyone reading them a story who actually knew how to read a story – dunno 'bout that. And big cheese's mom has now dubbed my non-Jewish Magical Scarecrows range the "You don't have to be Jewish Scarecrows" – which I think is the funniest thing ever and she (naturally) says she wants a Royalty for the idea– ha ha.
Signing off from Sydney :o))))))))) xxxxx

From: Lynn Santer
Sent: Wednesday, 25 August 2010 9:55 AM
To: Sandy
Subject: Did I tell you that I made Penthouse magazine?

Hi again,

Please find attached a story from Penthouse magazine on Alby, just FYI. In among his world death-defying adventures to exotic destinations, and his tireless efforts to help the planet and all its endangered wildlife, Alby is also somewhat notorious as a lady's man, hence Penthouse's interest in him. 90% of his fans are male from the "I wish I could live that life" category. As his official biographer I was included in the story (please see the last page) and I just think it's the funniest thing in the world that (a) I made Penthouse (b) with my clothes on, and (c) because of

Australia's most famous Lothareo……

When he became a recluse urban legends sprang up about him and there were regularly Elvis-type sightings. As you'll see, he became something of an icon, and in fact in complete contrast to Penthouse, the very high end, glossy, stylish magazine "Marie Claire" is also featuring him as their number one Australian icon in their forthcoming 15th anniversary edition, which is due out 30th August (in which I once again feature with him… hum… gonna start getting a rep for myself hey? Tee hee.)

Speak soon.
Luff & hugz,
The Kangaroo Kid… of Penthouse LOL

Are these the best signs in the whole world?

The next best-selling author?

Thought you'd find this cute, Sandy... As I may have mentioned, my Magical Scarecrows "Let's Make Magic for a Day" celebrity event for the disabled and disadvantaged children next year is, for the first time, taking place in conjunction with the RSPCA's Million Paws Walk (16th May). I am thrilled about this because it marries the principal behind my "Magical Scarecrow" stories about animals, with the children that the Magical Scarecrows philanthropic programs are focused at. As part of this the kids I support (from Leukaemia Foundation, Paradise Kids and Camp Quality) are all writing stories about their favourite animals and drawing pictures of them and these stories and drawings are forming the basis of a special edition Magical Scarecrows book that will be produced by me but sold by and for the RSPCA (Royal Society for the Prevention of Cruelty to Animals). This not only teaches children to think and write creatively, but it also encourages them with the knowledge that whatever their illness or ailment they can still contribute something positive to help someone else. Well, yesterday I received the entries from Paradise Kids (which is kids in crisis – they could be sick, abused, abandoned, etc). Of course they are all gorgeous but one in particular stood out, from 8 year old "Jack"....
I just thought that would put a smile on your face...

His favourite animal is a "Space Mouse". He's written an absolutely wonderful story about it and then added it's his favourite animal because (are you ready for this?) >>>

IT HASN'T BEEN INVENTED YET!!!!

You've just got to love that...:o)))))))))))))

Space Mice by Jack
Age 8

THE MAGICAL SCARECROWS SPECIAL RSPCA EDITION

Make magic with the

FOR THE MAGICAL SCARECROWS
"LET'S MAKE MAGIC" PROGRAM WITH THE
RSPCA'S "MILLION PAWS WALK" ~ 2010

AUNTIE LYNN

Mishaps, Mania
& Mischief Makers

From the "don't mess with me" collection

First a selection of emails directed at my client, Alby Mangels (an iconic folk hero in Australian circles) aimed to tarnish his name, written by someone (who clearly had no comprehension of who they were messing with) prompted by a story in NEW IDEA magazine about Alby's latest philanthropic efforts...

I should point out the emails FROM this chap were written in PINK Garmond font in a huge pitch!!! I have not attempted to clean up his spelling and grammatical mistakes, this is a direct quote:

We , and many others who knew Alby is at it again he took 100,s like me with his money making , and his so called helping the poor , it all went into his pocket, as for his Dog, you should know like we do he shot it himself, as he was going on one of his escapades and he could not find any one to look after it , so he said ,,OK and shot it ,, as for poor old Judy Green please get in touch with her she will blow your mind as how he destroyed her,and his RAPES of other, women, so your self beware , he will have YOU by the Crutch too. We are informing the Womens Magazine of the Whole affair. God what a laugh Mangles helping the poor ,, BEware Beware. Take Care.

My reply follows...

Dear Raymond,

Out of courtesy I am making you aware that your email has been put into the hands of our solicitors and the police.

For the record, I have known Alby for seven years and during that time I have never known him to be anything other than kind, considerate and giving. At all times he has treated me, my mother, my sister, my friends, and my colleagues with great respect.

For the record, I have not only met Judy Green but stayed in her home with her and her husband of over 20 years, Richard Norton, and am fully aware of the *real* truth behind her story. Alby did not destroy Judy, indeed Judy is far from destroyed. She was in an accident that was no one's fault, Alby paid for her medical care, he paid for her mother to fly to South America to be with her, he paid her handsomely for her role in World Safari II, and he kept *her* secrets quiet (which I am now fully aware of and have had these numerous secrets independently verified) demonstrating the true gentleman he is. Judy, like many others, fell in love with Alby – that was far from an exclusive club and hardly something Alby can be held responsible for.

For the record, I know the person who was looking after Sam when Alby went on his travels, He most assuredly did not shoot his dog.

For the record, it is interesting that it is a man who is accusing Alby of rape when NO woman EVER has. Where are these alleged rape victims? I would suggest they exist only in your mind. I have in fact heard from dozens of Alby's ex lovers since I have been managing his business and none have had a bad word to say about him, indeed the main reason for contact is that they want to see him again.

For the record, I should also make you aware that I have witnessed first hand Alby's benevolence to both animals and humans, and I am continuing to work closely with his sister on getting vital medical aid to a number of Third World countries – some of which I am personally taking to these countries myself – so you see Alby's contribution to the poor is very, very real and has been so for at least the entire seven years that I have known him.

For the record, the journalist from the Woman's Magazine you refer to has known Alby for five years and worked on no less than three stories with him during that time, and she too has seen with her own eyes the results of Alby's hands-on and financial philanthropic contributions to those less fortunate.

With these FACTS in mind what you have said amounts to actionable defamation and now you have made me aware in writing of your intent to slander my client's name I shall be instigating legal action for damages against you immediately in the new year if any further such communications come to my attention. Now you have made me aware of your intentions I shall know where to look first should any such erroneous allegations come to light, and have made the police aware of same as they are able to access your street address from this email address – which I thank you for supplying.

Most sincerely,
Lynn Santer
CC: Steven Prassas – Solicitor at law

He responded thus (errors deliberately not corrected)...

This response was written in the same Garamond font, same pitch as before, only this time in black:

Wow , This comes as a big surprise I got my comp back this morning to check on my emails, Who is this Manles fellow, never heard of him .
Also your intensions are way out,what are you seeking ,I am replying out of courtesy, As I never heard of your friend if this is a scam, then I will get in touch with the Police as to you infringing my my Privacy, people like you should get a job ,I am 80 years old and can do with out all this, I will inform you I was a Bench Magistrate before retiring 20 years ago, so, I will be getting legal council,.
Any one who would write to you using thier own address woukd be a fool, So I am cxspccting an apology.from who ever you are,. Raymond

I replied thus...

Nice try, Raymond, but…

1. Would a retired magistrate use the same (and quite uncommon) sized font as the original sender of the first email further down below?

2. Would a retired magistrate mix up the spelling of council (a government office) and counsel (as in legal counsel)?

3. Would a retired magistrate misspell such simple words as "their" and "expecting" and "would"?

4. Would a retired magistrate not be aware that there is nothing in my reply to an abusive email slandering my client that is even faintly actionable, never mind criminal?

5. Would a retired magistrate not know that the person who wrote the instigating abusive email slandering my client (with suspiciously matching poor grammar, spelling, punctuation and lay out to the instigating email) is seriously unlikely to have the nous to hack into someone else's email address – and in any event given the tone of instigating email why would the person attempt to disguise their true identity as they appeared to be quite proud of what they wrote and apparently wished to claim ownership of it. Perhaps you are suggesting that the person who was allegedly working on your computer (that you allege you only got back this morning) might have sent the email from your computer while they were working on it? If that is the case surely a retired magistrate would know better that to attempt to intimidate someone protecting their client and would surely rather be using their energy and focus in taking to task the individual you seem to be attempting to suggest might have sent an email from your computer while it was in the shop. A retired magistrate would, as I would do, be far more likely to write to me apologising that his name had been used illegally and assure the injured party (myself and my client) that this must have happened while the computer was with XYZ person and that they will be taking THAT person to the police – as this IS a criminal offence. This would appear to be a far more prudent and appropriate course of action for someone who understands the law.

6. In addition, your email is time-stamped at 9.17am – had you actually got your "comp back this morning" it must have been awfully early and you must have jumped on email awfully quickly.

I remain,
Your sincerely,
Lynn Santer
CC Steve Prassas – solicitor at law

And then... he went away ☺

BUT THAT'S NOT ALL!!!

What follows is the transcript of my conversation (under an assumed name) with another nutter out to tarnish my client... VERBATIM...

Me: This is Sandra Rasten - I'm a freelance journalist responding to your message
(NOTE: he was leaving messages for journalists all over town, and one of these called to advise me).

Mark: Oh - great!

Me: Can you tell me what these claims are you have against Alby Mangels?

Mark: Yes, yes. First of all there's crimes against humanity.

Me: Crimes against humanity. Really? What has he done that warrants this claim?

Mark: Well, his sister, Ria, called my home and was really rude to us.

Me: I see. Do you realise "crimes against humanity" generally refers to genocide?

Mark: What's genocide?
(Intake of breath by me - who on this planet does NOT know what genocide is??)

Me: The annihilation of an entire race.

Mark: Oh, well he might not have done that - but what would you call it?

Me: I'd call it a phone call, but let's move on. What else has he done?

Mark: Well there's the rape.

Me: Okay, tell me about that.
(Trying to sound calm and interested.)

Mark: This cop told me, nine months ago, Alby had been in jail for the past three months for rape.

Me: I see. What's the cop's name?
(Notwithstanding I knew exactly where Alby had been for the last twelve months, and it most definitely wasn't in jail!!)

Mark: I don't know his name.

Me: I see, this cop you don't know just volunteered this information to you out of the blue. Why would he do that?

Mark: I don't know. Maybe he felt sorry for me.

Me: I see, so this was some chap you met in a pub and were talking to about Alby?

Mark: It wasn't quite like that.

Me: What was it like?

Mark: Look, I don't know if that information was right, but he's definitely committed lots of rapes.

Me: Oh? There are other rapes you know of?

Mark: Yes, definitely.

Me: For instance?

Mark: Well, there's this girl who was a production assistant.

Me: What's her name?

Mark: I can't tell you that.

Me: Well how can I verify it's true if you can't tell me her name.

Mark: Okay her name is (*name deleted*). I know her quite well. She told me about her father who invented a new car engine but Ferrari stole it.
(Lynn thinks: okay - that sounds like a reliable witness - Ferrari stole her father's engine design - sure - oooooooooooo kkkkkkkkkkkkay)

Me: Ferrari stole the engine design from her father?

Mark: Yes, that's right.
(okay, good)

Me: And she was raped by Alby?

Mark: Yes, definitely – lots of times. Whenever she saw him.
(Me thinks: P-L-E-A-S-E……….."Lots of times" hey? Sounds more like "buyer's remorse" than rape to me.)

Me: What about your personal grievance with Alby. I believe you worked for him. When was that and doing what?

Mark: It was '93 - '96 - camera work and editing with Alby and Rick.

Me: And what happened?

Mark: They never paid me.

Me: They never paid you. That's it?

Mark: Yes, I'm owed 30% of all the films made in that time - 30% of $100 million.
(Oh good, Alby owes you $30 million – that's super – anyone would believe that – NOT!!!!!!!!!)

Me: I see. Do you have any documentation on that?

Mark: Well I made some notes.

Me: G-o-o-d, notes are splendid, but do you have any actual documentation? You know, like a contract?

Mark: Yes, yes, I have a contract between Alby and me.

Me: Good - can you email me that?
(Gave address in name of Sandra Rasten.)

Mark: Yes, I can scan it and do that.
(Still waiting – like that's ever gonna happen.)

Me: Thank you. And can I have your email address?

Mark: Yes: (email address provided)
(Quick search - no company registered in that name.)

Me: And what have you been doing since 1996?

Mark: Trying to get justice.

Me: I see – that's nice, but I meant work wise.

Mark: I haven't had time to work. I've been busy trying to get justice - dealing with lawyers - that's why I'm broke.

Me: I see. Which lawyers have you been dealing with?

Mark: I can't remember.

Me: You can't remember which lawyers you've been dealing with for the last fourteen years?
(!!!!!!!!!!!!!!!!!!!!!!!!!)

Mark: Well there was David.

Me: Do you have his phone number?

Mark: No. He's dead.
(Of course he is!!!!!!!!)

Me: Okay. Any other lawyers?

Mark: Well there will be when you pay me for the story. *(Yeah – that'll happen............ when hell freezes over!!!!!!!)*

Me: So you haven't worked in the last fourteen years?

Mark: Well on and off. I haven't really had time and then there was the police raid.

Me: What police raid?

Mark: The CIB raided my home - they were dirty cops working for Alby and stole (seized) all my VHS tapes of the films we made together.

Me: The CIB were working for Alby?
(This just gets better and better really, doesn't it? I don't think I could write a fantasy script like this!!!!!!!! The CIB work for Alby... excellent.)

Mark: That's right. A dirty cop.

Me: Do you have a name?

Mark: John Van (deleted) - he's retired now.

Me: Have you spoken to any other media about this?

Mark: Yes.

Me: Who?

Mark: The LA Times, New York Times, Sunday Mail and the Melbourne office of Today Tonight.

Me: You've spoken with all those people?

Mark: I left messages for them all.

Me: Have any of them called you back?

Mark: No, not yet.
(Go figure that!)

So let us recap:

1. A "rude" phone call from **RIA** means ALBY has "committed crimes against humanity" – excellent.
2. Alby was in jail at the time of this call for rape – marvellous – given I know exactly where he was at the time of this call – and it most certainly wasn't jail!!!!!!!!!
3. This information was imparted by a "cop" whose name this Mark doesn't even know – yeah that's very credible.
4. Alby raped this woman "lots of times" – she must have liked it a lot to keep going back for more!!!!!!!!!!!!! But then she did tell Mark that Ferrari stole her father's engine design, so the poor love would have been understandably distraught – first Ferrari raped her dad and then Alby rapes her – repeatedly on lots of occasions – it's a tragedy really!!!!!!!!!!
5. The CIB work for Alby – just love that one!!!!!!!
6. He can't remember the names of lawyers he's worked with for FOURTEEN years – except the one who died – splendid!!!!!!!!!
7. He hasn't worked for fourteen years because he's been too busy with all these lawyers whose names he can't remember and that's why he's broke – oh sure THAT IS why he's broke!!!!
8. And let's not forget the doozy of Alby owes him $30 million – MARVELLOUS STUFF – oh yeah, this guy's gonna come across really credible.

He kept asking what he'd be paid for the story. I promised I wouldn't print anything without discussing it with him first. I didn't lie!!!!!!!! HE MIGHT BE WAITING A WHILE!!!

Alfred Dunhill

From: Lynn Santer
Sent: Monday, 1 June 2009 4:21 PM
To: jason.scott.XXXXX@alfreddunhill.xxx.xx
Cc: xxxx@cigarworld.xxx.xx; **Subject:** Dunhill lighter service
Importance: High

Dear Jason,

Let me begin by saying that I have always received the utmost sterling service from Trent at Cigar World on the Gold Coast. He has at all times been charming, accommodating, and extremely knowledgeable about the product. The reason for this missive is because we have reached a situation where my lighters require a service that, for no reason of Trent's, Cigar World is unable to provide.

I have two gold Dunhill lighters, one of which is particularly precious to me not only because it is 40 years old but because it belonged to my beloved late father. When I lived in London getting these lighters serviced never presented even the merest hint of a problem, yet here in Queensland it seems it would be easier to relocate Mt Everest to a crater on Mars and only then attempt to summit it.

To begin with Trent did the very best he could to service both lighters, which inexplicably both stopped working at the same time. Then began the saga. As you would be well aware, despite Trent's knowledge and expertise he is not an authorised Dunhill repair person and hence the necessary parts are not available to him. Indeed I have been advised by Richemont Australia that they are not available in the whole of this continent! The rigmarole required to get so much as a quote is ridiculous in the extreme, taking an inordinate amount of time during which items of both financial and emotional value are not only out of one's possession but out of the country! Again, in London all I needed to do was pop into the local shop and a service was conducted while I waited! I have been advised now I live in Australia I would be lucky to have my lighters back in my hands inside TWO MONTHS from sending them to Richemont for a quote… that's if I could even get them there.

When I called Australia Post to inquire about insuring the items for postage to Sydney from Queensland I was advised I could not even mail used lighters because they are classified as dangerous goods. Richemont told me I could mail them if I did as they did, and that is to not insure them but merely register them, which does not require declaring what the contents are. However, as I stated, these are not only items of financial value, my father's lighter is also an item of extreme personal value and there is no way I am letting it out of my possession uninsured.

I have no doubt Alfred Dunhill would be turning in his grave if he were aware of the utter lack of customer service being provided to Australia, and especially Australians based outside of Sydney, clientele of his fine old establishment which prided itself not only in fine quality goods, but also fine quality customer service. "Service" in this instance is hardly an adjective that could reasonably be attributed to the sequence of events detailed above without placing a greater burden on the etymology of the word than it could reasonably be expected to bear. Is this what your company has been reduced to? It would be a sad reflection on the fine history of this grand establishment if so.

Awaiting the kind favour of your swift and well-considered reply.

Your sincerely,
Lynn Santer

Sent: 06/19/2009 07:58 AM ZE10
To: 'Cigarworld Australia'; Jason Scott-xxxx
Subject: Thank you

Dear Trent and Jason,

Please convey my thanks up, down, and across the line for the prompt, courteous, and efficient service I have now received in getting both my lighters repaired. Mr Dunhill Snr would be proud. ☺

I'm sorry it took what it took but it shows what can be done. Incredibly it turned out that both lighters had exactly the same problem (very strange). Even more remarkably, according to all the testimony I received from everyone involved, the parts necessary to fix the problems were in stock in Sydney! From leaving the Cartier boutique in Surfers Paradise until receiving the lighters back in working order, delivered to my door step, took only one week! Perhaps you only tell clients it takes 2-3 months so we are overly impressed with you when a week's turnaround is in fact possible, n'est pas? TEE HEE LOL

The ladies in Cartier couldn't have been nicer, and were rewarded with a modest sale for their efforts, and the ladies in Richemont positively fell over themselves with customer service, communication and attention that was indeed second to none!

You have a very happy client here

Good things always,
Lynn Santer aka "Auntie Lynn"

Festive Funnies

Despite the sore heads, and a glutton-sized belly,
Or perhaps you have simply been in front of the telly,
Whatever your penchant, whatever your heart's desire,
May it blossom and bloom with passionate fire.

The old year is over, a new start awaits,
Grab it with both hands before it's too late.
Before we all know it, it will be Christmas again,
Be sure when that happens you stand out among men.

Be successful, be happy, be of good health and good cheer,
As with great joy and optimism we welcome this year.
You are special in spirit, and special to me,
So please accept this wish as it's sent, with sincere love to
thee!

My Wish for You in 2007

**May peace break into your house and may thieves come
to steal your debts. May the pockets of your jeans
become a magnet for $100 bills. May love stick to your
face like Vaseline and may laughter assault your lips!
May your clothes smell of success like smoking tyres
and may happiness slap you across the face and may
your tears be that of joy. May the problems you had
forget your home address! In simple words ....
May 2007 be the best year of your life!!!**

**HERE'S TO THE YEAR OF OO7 – LICENSED TO
THRILL!!!!!!!!!! HAPPY NEW YEAR!!!!!!!!!!**

On the last working day of this action-packed year,
I'm thinking of you and I'm filled with good cheer,
I can't help but wonder with a smile on my face,
How grand that it is you've come into my space.
Joyous times are upon us and a new year awaits,
So looking back I must say, "IT'S JUST BEEN SO
GREAT
That you are a part of my life and there is no denying,
Our paths crossed for a reason and when things are
trying,
I know that I'm richer because our paths have crossed,
And in the year that unfolds that fact will not be lost!!!"

MERRY EVERYTHING!!!!!!!!!!!

HUGZ FROM SANTER CLAWS 2007

From: Lynn Santer
Sent: Saturday, December 25, 2010 04:56 AM
To: 'Anita Herrick/Tippi Hedren'
Subject: The perfect Christmas cake

It's almost 5am Christmas morning and the household's asleep - all except for mutant Santer whose email can't keep!!!

Cry laughing – I did!!!!!!!! CHERRY NISTMAS FROM SANTER CLAWS xxxxxxxxxxxx

Ingredients for **THE CAKE YOU DRINK....**
1 cup of water
1 tsp baking soda
1 cup of sugar
1 tsp salt
1 cup of brown sugar
Lemon juice
4 Large eggs
Nuts
1 Bottle of Vodka
2 cups of dried fruit

Method:
Sample the vodka to check quality. Take a large bowl check the vodka again.

To be sure it is the highest quality, pour one level cup and drink.

Repeat.

Turn on the electric mixer. Beat one cup of butter in a large fluffy bowl.

Add one teaspoon of sugar. Beat again.

At this point it's best to make sure the vodka is shtill OK.

Try another cup, just in case turn off the mixerer.

Break 2 leggs and add to the bowl and chuck in the cup of dried fruit.

Pick fruit off floor.

Mix on the turner.

If the fried druit gets stuck in the beaterers pry it loose with a sdrewscriver.

Sample the vodka to check for tonsisticity.

Next, sift two cups of salt. Or something. Who giveshz a poo.

Check the vodka.

Now shift the lemon juice and strain your nuts.

Add one table.

Add a spoon of sugar, or somefink. Whatever you can find.

Greash the oven and piss in the fridge.

Turn the cake tin 360 degrees and try not to fall over.

Don't forget to beat off the turner.

Finally, throw the bowl through the window, finish the vodka and kick the cat.

Fall into bed.

CHERRY MISTMAS!
**NOW THAT'S WHAT I CALL A NISTMAS
CAKE!!!!!!!!!!!!**

Animal Antics

"The Birds"...

From: Lynn Santer
Sent: Sunday, October 24, 2004 8:26pm
To: Anita Herrick/Tippi Hedren
Subject: Baby Crows

Tippi!!!

A pair of crows have made a nest in one of the palm trees right by our swimming pool... and Mrs Crow is currently sitting on eggs = :o))))

Hd to tell you!
Hugz
The Kangaroo Kid xxxxx

8th November, 2004, 9:31pm

Tippi/Anita!!!

The rains stopped for a while today and mom and dad crow took the three kids out to show them how to fly. Le Santers du lak (Santers of the lake) happened to be passing the bay window at the time. All tools du jour were instantly downed and we sat and watched... and watched... and watched. >>>

"Here," squawked mommy crow from the stratosphere. "This is how it's done."

Daddy crow watched on with admiration while the three kids just looked bemused.

"Oy vey," said daddy crow (Jewish crow!!) "Okay, kids, LOOK… this is how we do it…" and dad took off into the stratosphere.

"Er, bro, did ya see what mom and dad just did?" asked kid crow # 1. "Don't look too safe to me. I'm high tailing it back to the nest."

And he did.

That left two.

Closer and closer the remaining two came to the edge of the palm leaf.

Closer and closer le Santers du lak came to the edge of their chairs.

They flapped their wings.

We held our breath.

"Oh shit! This is too hard," squawked crow kid # 2. "And anyhow, it's beginning to rain again."

There will now be a brief pause…………………

That was it… LOL.

This process was repeated.

We topped up wine glasses. >>>

We waited.

All three crow kids slowly crept to the end of the branch again.

The big wimp crow kid thought better of the whole procedure and leap-frogged (leap-crowed?) his siblings to return to the nest once more… which actually necessitated becoming airborne, albeit very briefly. YAHOO!!!

"Some on," le Santers du lak cried. "You're born to do it… just FLY!!"

Hummmmmmmmmm……… waiting…………………

Still waiting……………………….

Flapping… drinking… parental aerial acrobatics…. Squawestruck… edging to the end of the palm leaf… edging to the end of our chairs… will they? Won't they? Where's the Bourbon???

And finally… airborne avian antics… they all took flight! We nearly cried! We didn't. We poured champagne instead LOL (any excuse!!!)

Just knew you'd love to know.
Big hugz from Oz,
The Kangaroo Kid :o)))))))))) xxxxxxxxx

Australia's funniest home video?

From: Lynn Santer
Sent: Monday, May 03, 2004 2:16pm
To: Mum Santer

Okay, last night was one for the video camera – shame it wasn't running. After a peaceful day of working on my latest book without incident, down here on my sister's farm in beautiful rural Victoria, sister Karen collected my nephews from school and went into the City for her evening shift at the law firm. My instructions were pretty simple: feed the boys, feed the dogs, try not to kill anything, and get the ducks and geese put away. It was the latter that proved to be somewhat entertaining…

"Just open their pen, walk up to them quietly, and they'll just go in. The boys can help you," my sister advised me.

The operative word here was "quietly". Have you ever met one little boy, never mind two, capable of "quietly"???

So when the appointed time came, I asked the boys if they'd give me a hand. They enthusiastically agreed, descending on these poor birds as though it was the clash of the Titans! Geese were honking, ducks were quacking, boys were screaming, feathers were flying, and this was all too much for the dogs to resist!

So… adding barking dogs into this equation, Auntie Lynn decided it was time to divest herself of a few layers to be dexterous enough to deal with the situation (remember the man on the radio this morning said it was so cold he just saw four penguins walking past in mink coasts!!!!)

Trying to prioritize in an orderly fashion, as is my way, the first job was to get the dogs penned up where they >>>

could cause no further mayhem. I considered penning the boys up with them, but I've seen how easily they can climb out, so that really seemed a moot point.

Then Joshua caught one of the ducks – great! So that was put to bed, and I shut the gate. As Lachlan and I chased after the geese, Josh very helpfully opened the gate to allow the geese to go in, which – you've guessed – meant the duck rushed out again!!! It was a bit like one of those games where you try to get the balls in the holes without disturbing the balls that you've already secured!!

If your sides are splitting and the tears are rolling down your cheeks, that's nothing to what it was actually like here! Can you imagine the musical backing that would accompany this fiasco? I imagine something from one of the old Benny Hill shows.

Finally the boys and I formed what I've seen cheetah coalitions do in Africa – surrounded the frantic feathers from three different angles in a coordinated attack. This was ultimately successful… and I have this little game to look forward to tomorrow and Wednesday nights as well! Are we having fun yet??

Yours with love,
Auntie Lynn… missing my manicures!!!
Hugz,
Grins and giggles :o)))))))) xxxxxxx

Dinner with Ro (email to Tippi)

Hi there,

You know I love living in paradise on the Gold Coast…I do… truly I do… but summer has come early and with a vengeance this year, and with it some of the downsides to living in this place such as bushfires and… SPIDERS!!!

Honestly, if it swims, slithers, crawls or flies and it's deadly – it lives in Australia. That's not to take away for a moment from the beauty, the tranquility, the freedom, and so on, but Aussies do have a funny sense of what's harmful and what's not. I guess because there are so many deadly creatures, the attitude is, "What doesn't kill you is harmless". There is, in fact, a very large shade of grey between deadly and harmless, and one such example is the huntsman spider…

Aside from the fact that this huge lumbering beast could terrify you to death by the mere sight of it, its bite is sufficient to make one quite ill. Why am I telling you this? Read on…

The other night I spent the evening with Ro London (the lady who designed the outfit I wore to the Emmys last month) in her magnificent 70 square/2 acre home. We were happily sipping champagne (of course we were) engaged in good girlie gossip, when a reasonable specimen of a huntsman came scurrying across the wall. We were both on our feet in an instant.

"I'll spray it," said Ro.

"That's a waste of time," I replied, having witnessed vain efforts to spray these giant beasts in the past. They merely cough it off and get angry! Besides, I prefer to capture >>>

them and release them alive if possible.

Ro accepted my suggestion and searched for a dish/pot/bucket large enough to capture the eight-legged monster in. Clearly it heard us. Okay, I know that's not possible, but perhaps it picked up a vibe? I dunno, but whatever the reason it scuttled behind a plant to hide. Hummmmmmmmmmm…

"No problem," said Ro. "The urn (in which said plant was contained) is on wheels. I'll move it."

The urn moved… the spider moved… the girls moved… oh dear! The next phase was for said eight-legged monster to run to the highest corner of the wall where we could neither spray it or capture it! Rats!!! Or in this case… spiders!!! Why did it have to be spiders???

We had another glass of champagne (always a good idea) and tried to remain calm as we continued our conversation as though nothing was wrong…

Then it disappeared! That's worse!!! Where the heck was it???

We decided to clear up the dishes. Ro headed to the dishwasher, opened it, and out jumped one eight-legged dog's mother!!! Holy c*!^(!#&p!!!!! You should have seen the size of this thing!!! This time we sprayed (don't go lurking in ambush to pounce on us you bleep, bleep, bleep!). It ran back inside the dishwasher. We shut it and put it on. There were no dishes in it, just one eight-legged horse (you do notice how it's growing as this story continues?).

Hearts thudding…

>>>

We ran upstairs and decided to barricade ourselves into our respective bedrooms for the night, hoping our dreams wouldn't be dominated by recent events. In the cold hard morning light things might seem better. Sure enough, now I sit in my office writing this missive, safely back at home, I feel much better. Oh wait… Holy c**!!##$!*&#p!!! No I don't!! You will NOT believe this….

Guess who is watching me write to you?

COUSIN OF EIGHT LEG!!! Blinking heck!!!! It's sitting on my office wall sizing me up for lunch!!!

Gotta go………

Hugz from Oz,
The Kangaroo Kid ☺ xxxxxxxx

We're parents!!!! (Email to Tippi)

Dateline 31st July, 2004…

The swans on the lake in our back garden have just given birth to five little baby fluff ball swanettes (that might be cygnets).

Daddy swan is being VERY protective (he was up on the street and nearly ate Chelsea when I took her for a walk this morning!!!). We are so excited and thrilled – and more excited – I wanted to share the news with you.

What a wonderful way to start the day.

More on the swans

Dateline 5th August, 2004…

I hate to tell you this but there are only two babies left from the five. Two just disappeared very early on, and the third – OMG…

My neighbour called me in an absolute flap. She could see it dying in the nest. I raced out. Mum and dad and the two surviving babies were all in my garden, and the third was gasping in the nest. I raced back in, pulled on a cossie, and raced back out, diving into the lake to swim across to it. It's winter here. FAR OUT… IT WAS COLD!!!! My neighbour has a tiny boat that her husband uses on the lake. Lady neighbour can't drive it, and I have to tell you… neither can I! I have never attempted to row a boat in my life. Nonetheless, it was a better option that swimming in the freezing water, so I hopped in and got it going. I couldn't stop it or turn it around, but I got it going, calling, "Hey, where's the brakes on this thing?" from the deepest part of the lake.

When I arrived at the nest the third baby was already gone. We were all just devastated (half of the street was out by this stage). I guess we have to accept this is the natural order of things and not all offspring from a big brood are going to make it. His little spark of life has entered the universal pool from where he can watch his brothers and sisters perpetuate the species. It's survival of the fittest, but on a happier note, the swans do seem to know that we care. Mom and dad will bring the babies (only days old) right up to us, and they didn't try to stop me from helping when I was getting near the nest.

People say animals aren't self-aware and don't have feelings. What idiots those people are! There was >>>

a bit of trash in the lake yesterday and one of the babies tried to eat it (as any baby would do). I yelled, "NO!" and daddy swan got all hissy at me, flapping his wings because I'd shouted. So… I pointed to the piece of trash the baby was trying to eat. He looked down, picked it up, and threw it out of the way!!! Don't tell me these animals aren't thinking, feeling, intelligent creatures!!!

With love,
The Kangaroo Kid… with swan…

May the footprints you leave behind show you walked in kindness to all living things.

Even more on the swans!!!

Dateline 16th April, 2005…

They've nested again!!! This time in total secrecy. Last week they produced a new brood and this morning they bought their new little fluff balls to meet me. What a perfectly delightful way to start this Sunday!!! Mum, dad, and the kids all ate right from my hand (healthy food for swans… and normally I leave them to eat only what's naturally in the lake). But we had an interloper… Cheeky… the Moor Hen with attitude…

Cheeky was jumping up and down on feet, scratching my legs, and used absolutely shocking language for a young bird, complaining about the whole thing (he is just SO cute!!!). It was in fact quite a gathering this morning: white ducks, pacific black ducks, moor hens, coots, and even Harry (the friendly pelican that thinks it's a Labrador). They were all behaving perfectly beautifully, getting along in a very civilised fashion until Cheeky decided he'd had enough of all this attention going to the swans and the little shit PECKED ME!!! How rude.

As my encounter with the swans drew to a close, and I watched them glide gracefully away, Cheeky actually climbed up my leg… with his claws (ouch!!) flapping his wings to balance as he climbed!! What the????

Now, Tippi, what was the name of that film you made with Hitchcock again? LOL.

Hugz from Oz,
The Kangaroo Kid ☺ xxxxxxx

Yeah, men… they are animals and hence should be in this section too, right?

READ BEFORE OPENING PHOTO:

BE AFRAID... BE VERY AFRAID...

This is one of the more fascinating e-mails I've seen for a while. As the text says - "Nature can be cruel, however there is a raw beauty in it all". Be careful of those around you when you do open it as I'm sure not all will appreciate it in the same way I think you will.......At times nature can be cruel, but there is also a raw beauty, and even a certain justice manifested within that cruelty.

The croc, one of the oldest and ultimate predators, normally considered the "apex predator", can still fall victim to implemented 'team work' & strategy, made possible due to the tight knit social structure and "survival of the pack mentality" bred into the canines.

See the remarkable photograph attached, courtesy of Nature Magazine.

Note that the Alpha dog has a muzzle hold on the crocodile preventing it from breathing, while another dog has a hold on the tail to keep it from thrashing. The third dog attacks the soft underbelly of the croc.

The eight-legged dog

We have a giant resident spider who has got into the very annoying habit of building Buckingham Web across our driveway during the summer. Only it seems to have forgotten to hibernate during this winter (or "carbonate" as Olga's Russian translation calls it LOL). When I realized that Deidre would be arriving from Melbourne late and in the dark, and knowing she hadn't been here before and therefore wouldn't be aware of Buckingham Web, I decided to take measures to make the web visible so she wouldn't walk into it. You'll understand I didn't want to disturb our resident or break her web, so I came up with the brainwave of decorating the web with curling ribbon!!! Really!!!! Well, you wouldn't doubt me, would you? Just in case… check out the photo below. I think it came out rather well actually. I did feel a little guilty (well, I am Jewish!!!) when I placed the first piece of ribbon as Ms Charlotte (all spiders are called Charlotte, aren't they??) raced over thinking prey had landed in her loom… but she took one mouthful and said (I heard her, I swear!!)… she said, "Poo yukky, what's that?" and returned to her central pouncing position. When the second and third pieces of ribbon went up she just ignored them and remained resolute in the centre of the web. Who knows, perhaps she even thought her web looked rather pretty???
You're laughing, aren't you???

Deidre duly arrived with a chilled bottle of Moet in hand and was barely even surprised… well, she has known me for over 20 years.

Off to take aspirin now…
All good things, "Auntie Lynn"… **PHOTO FOLLOWS…**

Look what happened this morning!!! That's a
kookaburra on our patio, and me feeding it with a plate
of minced meat... look on....

Isn't he lovely??? And SO TAME – ATE RIGHT OUT
OF MY HAND!!!!!!

From: Lynn Santer
Sent: Thursday, June 24, 2010 3:10 PM
To: 'Anita Herrick/Tippi Hedren'
This is a hold up... Your bread roll or else!!

Back in 2001 Tippi may remember going to Currumbin
wildlife sanctuary where we had a press call with Tippi and
"The Birds", beautiful rainbow lorikeet parrots who fly in
twice daily to be fed. Well, yesterday I took mom there for
lunch (which is not feeding time for the birds – they are fed
at 8am and 4pm). You can just go to the sanctuary for
lunch now without paying entry to the wildlife park.
Anyway, there we were having a quiet little repast when a
sole rainbow lorikeet came and sat in front of us demanding
to be fed (he was really quite cheeky LOL). Silly (and
naughty) mom broke off a crumb from her roll to give to
said lorikeet. I thoroughly disapproved (a) because bread
isn't good for them and (b) because, as I said, "Er, mom...
remember where you are!" Sure enough, one tweet later,
and there were two dozen lorikeets on our table, all
assertively demanding our lunches be handed over
immediately!

Half laughing and half overwhelmed by their demanding
attitude, mom threw both halves of her bread roll onto the
far corner of our table. The gathered tweety throng duly
congregated in an orderly fashion around the two halves of
bread roll, quietly munching away, until one decided it was
thirsty after all that pecking and hopped up onto mom's
glass of water! She gasped and complained, waving her
hands, which only served to send said thirty demanding
lorikeet towards my glass. I gently attempted to push him
away and the cheeky little shit bit me!!!! Okay, fine,
you're thirsty – I get it. So I opened my bottle of water and
put the lid upside down on the table while he waited and
watched apparently fully aware of what I was about to do.

>>>

I filled the lid with water and he was perfectly happy to drink away from that… until the rest of the flock decided that was rather a good idea too!!! Oy vey – honestly!!!!

I tried to line up a few of them on my arm to wait their turn. They were happy enough to hop onto my arm but became bored very quickly when they discovered there was nothing to eat or drink up there. Other patrons, and even Currumbin staff, were watching the cabaret having hysterics – no one attempted to step in!!!

Just thought you'd appreciate the little anecdote xxxxxxx

From: Anita Herrick
Sent: Friday, 25 June 2010 8:22 AM
To: 'Lynn Santer'
Subject: RE: The birds

Hi Lynn,

That is so funny!!! I have copied it to give to Tippi…

Anita

From: Lynn Santer
Sent: Sunday, August 01, 2010 2:36 PM
To: Anita Herrick/Tippi Hedren
Subject: Just not her cup of tea

Dearest Tippi and Anita,

Funniest thing I've ever seen… there I was having a
morning cuppa on the balcony, watching pretty little Mrs
Dove sit down calmly on the balustrade serenely watching
the world go by, when randy Mr Dove flew in to settle by
her side. Ah… how nice. Said Mr Dove then clearly felt
like a little morning glory and began cooing and dancing
his very best dance replete with courtship head bopping
gestures. Mrs Dove turned around, looked him up and
down… and flew off. I spat a mouthful of coffee across the
table laughing (admittedly all the while feeling a little sorry
for the unrequited love of poor Mr Dove).
Happy day xxxxxxxxxxx

Extract from my biography "An Unbelievable Life" by Sandra L. Rogers, available from Zeus Publications

My very first encounter with the eight-legged beast of Oz...

By 1980 Clare (Lynn's mum) was tiring of all Neville's intercontinental business travel and suggested he buy a retail pharmacy, thinking this might tie him to home and hearth. After having been connected to the Santer genes for so long one could have been forgiven for thinking Clare should have known better. He purchased the retail pharmacy, as she wished, but retained his position as Managing Director of Norgine Pharmaceuticals Australasia, ultimately becoming their Chairman. Far from running the pharmacy, Neville appointed the newly qualified Lynn as shop manager (aged 19) to support the qualified pharmacist, Jenny, who ran the dispensary. Clare was left busying herself as part-time sale assistant.

The shop, Maxwell's Pharmacy, had been established for 100 years, the building itself reminiscent of an old time apothecary with twenty-foot high ceilings, in the bustling hub of Chapel Street in the Melbourne suburb of Prahran. The business had the pharmaceutical contract for the Freemason's Homes, which meant the person who purchased it from old Mr Maxwell didn't only have to be a pharmaceutical chemist (by law) but also a Freemason in order to retain that lucrative side of the operation. Both Neville and his father before him had been members of this powerful fraternity, so the deal was sealed.

In addition to the pills and potions that needed to be dispensed on a daily basis for the Freemason's contract, old Mr Maxwell had built up an eclectic mix of faithful clientele, among them some extremely colourful characters. Lynn remembered one particular woman who wore a bucket on her head, daily changing the sticky contact film on it to pretty flowery patterns that matched whatever outfit she was wearing that day. There was another lady who would come in, raise her arms to heaven, holler some indiscernible non-existent language, and then buy three packets of barley sugar. And there was the local neighbourhood optometrist, whose real name she can't recall but whom she nicknamed 'Glum' from 'Gulliver's Travels'. This man never knew how to smile and whatever words left his lips were always of doom and gloom.

Despite being excited about her new life in Australia there was one prospect of life on this South Pacific continent that filled her with utter dread ... spiders! Back in the UK she had been frightened of even the smallest spiders, and they weren't poisonous. She swore, the first time she saw a large spider in Australia she would be heading out to the airport, getting on the next plane, wherever it might take her, and never coming back. Well, that day came at Maxwell's Pharmacy.

After arriving in Australia Lynn quickly learned that Australians have a strange sense of what is dangerous and what isn't. She guessed this must be because per capita of population, or per square inch of land, however you measured it, Australia has more deadly creatures than anywhere else on earth. If it crawls, slithers, swims or flies, and it's deadly – it lives in Australia. In England she knew 'spider'. Once in Australia she quickly learned their individual names, ranks and serial numbers. She could instantly identify a red back from a golden orb from a huntsman or a funnel web, white tail, St Andrew's cross ... and she could tell you how venomous or not they were too. She isn't quite sure when or how this happened, she just realised one day her knowledge of arachnids had expanded exponentially. She assumed because there were so many creatures in Australia that can kill you the attitude of most Australians was that if it can't kill you then it's harmless. What rubbish! There's a huge shade of grey between deadly and harmless, and anything that can cause physical pain, injury, or make you sick is far from harmless. The huntsman spider falls into that latter category.

Lynn was helping Jenny out in the dispensary one day. Jenny was the so-called 'spinster' pharmacist who had worked at Maxwell's Pharmacy since long before the Santer's took ownership and thought she at least part-owned the place herself. She was an extremely knowledgeable and efficient pharmacist but outside of her life in Maxwell's she was the sort of lady who preferred spiders to men. Anyway ... the security beam at the front of the store was broken and the familiar buzz told Lynn a customer was in the store. She wandered out to serve the customer, for some reason glancing up to the twenty-foot ceiling ... and there it was ... the biggest arachnid Lynn had ever seen in her life!

Swallowing the scream that was choking in her throat she served the customer, all the time keeping one eye on the beast which looked as big as a dinner plate to her. The moment Jenny and Lynn were once again alone she released the scream with all the velocity that had gathered in the pent-up moments serving the customer. Frantically asking her what was wrong; Jenny collapsed laughing when Lynn pointed a shaking and accusing finger towards the ceiling.

"Oh, is that all?" Jenny scoffed.

"All?" Lynn gasped. "Do you see the size of that thing?"

"So what?" she quaffed. "What are you going to do about it?"

"This is a pharmacy," Lynn blurted, a little exasperated by Jenny's attitude. "There must be something in that dispensary of yours, um, excuse me, of OURS, that we can use to, well, dispense of this creature."

"Oh, leave it alone. It will go away."

"Go away? That's just great! And which bottle will I find it behind? What if it leaps out at a customer?"

Ignoring Lynn as if she were a petulant child, Jenny returned to the sanctuary of her dispensary, leaving our heroine alone with the beast. Lynn glanced up at it once more. Not that she knew much about the behaviour of arachnids, but to her it seemed to be asleep; inactive with one 'tentacle' kinda sticking out. Marching into the dispensary, Lynn slumped down in a chair and huffed at Jenny, who was still ardently ignoring her. Whilst scrutinising the shelves, she came up with plan after plan to deal with the dreaded nemesis.

"Arsenic!" she blurted.

"What?" Jenny blinked.

"I'll get up there with an eye dropper and feed it some arsenic."

"Not on my watch you won't," Jenny thundered.

Lynn huffed again.

"I'll throw a brick at it!"

"Oh really?" Jenny drawled. "I can see it now. You'll end up on the floor with the brick on you, and the spider on the brick laughing its head off."

She huffed again, determined not to be defeated, gradually hatching a rather brilliant plan.

Moments later Clare arrived. Quickly she brought her mother up to date with the occurrences and advised her of the brilliant plan. Moments after that 'Glum' arrived. He glanced up at the ceiling, looked Lynn dead in the eyes, and said in his standard voice of doom, "There's enough venom in that to make the lot of youse sick for a week!"

"That's it!" Lynn snapped. "It has to go."

This was a colourful operation. While assessing the potions and mixtures on the pharmacy shelves Lynn had drawn the conclusion that one extremely expensive cough mixture, was going to be the key ingredient. The mixture was lobelia (which is bright green) and 33% ether. Knowing nothing whatsoever about the pharmacology behind this her uninformed brain told her that 33% ether was probably enough to knock out a spider while not knocking her out at the same time. Of course Lynn gave no regard whatsoever to the fact that Jenny was accountable for every drop of controlled medicine in the establishment, nor did she have the slightest knowledge of the respiratory system of arachnids.

Lynn grabbed a large wad of cotton wool, waited until Jenny had to answer a technical question for a customer (and hence leave the dispensary unguarded), then wrapped the cotton wool around a ten-foot pole (which was bright red), that they'd used for window displays during the Christmas season, took possession of an empty tin of 5,000 Panadol (which was silver) and donned thick rubber gloves (which were bright blue). Armed with a ladder mother and daughter headed into the store to action their plan.

When Jenny saw this colourful parade marching out of her domain she enquired as to what on earth we were up to.

"Don't worry," Lynn told her. "I'm not going to hurt it, it's only ether."

"It's what?" Jenny growled.

It was Lynn's turn to ignore Jenny, instructing her mum to climb up the ladder until the red pole with the green-soaked cotton wool at the end of it could be shoved up the spider's nose. She only later learned (with some sadness, because she didn't really want to actually kill the creature, she just wanted it somewhere, anywhere, else) that ether is lethal to spiders … even 33%. She thought the spider would pass out and could be scooped up with her gloves, put in the big Panadol tin and taken outside to scamper off. That's not what happened.

The spider seemed to go on some kind of high, and actually clung onto the cotton wool. Clare gently lowered the pole and Lynn did manage to successfully secure it in the tin and take it outside, but that poor spider didn't live to see another day. It shrivelled and died in a dark corner only minutes later. Lynn believes that, when she next used that ladder and pole to decorate the window for Christmas, had an accident, lost her footing and went tumbling backwards off the ladder into the window, was fitting retribution. At the time there was a lot of blood and many fist-sized bruises. It wasn't until years later she discovered the full extent of more serious injuries.

As a result of that accident Lynn had damaged her spine in five places: one at the base of the spine, two in between her shoulder blades, and two in the back of her neck. With increasing years other developments have brought those injuries to the fore. While, for the most part, she lives a perfectly normal and pain-free life there are occasions when a turn the wrong way, sitting for too long in front of the computer, or simply turning her head around in the car to reverse will forever remind her of that moment.

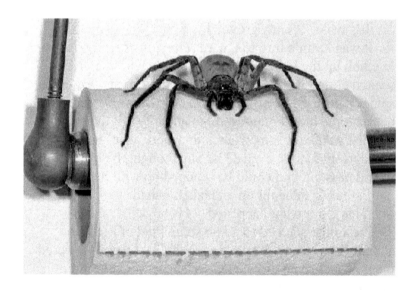

THE NEPHEWS

From: Lynn Santer
Subject: Report on visiting nephews
To: Karen.oBrien
Date: Saturday, January 19, 2008, 2:04 PM

Hey Sis,

First of all I was peacefully taking a shower the other day
and reached down to pick up a bottle of shampoo.
Somewhat horrified I discovered an eight-legged dog had
grabbed hold of it first and was prepared to challenge me
for possession!!! Being in mid-shower is a bit like being in
mid-pee or mid-… whatever… I really didn't want to stop
until I'd finished, so keeping one eye fervently soap free,
and widely open, I keenly focused my vision on this eight-
legged monster (who seemed to be rather enjoying the
shower actually, occasionally stretching out a tendril to
reach under one of its multiple armpits… I genuinely had
visions of it unscrewing the shampoo bottle and lathering
up its hair covered body!) until I had cleansed my own cute
little body (??!!) with extreme caution and care, wrapped
myself in a bath towel, and called to the boys (who were
ensconced watching cartoons) to come and see today's
SHOW AND TELL. There were "oos" and "ahs" and "oh
gee, Auntie Lynn, that's a really big spider!" Yeah, no
sh*t!!!!!!!!!!!

After the obligatory consternation that followed I captured
this eight-legged horse (yes, it grew while the debate on
removal was occurring… well of course it did!!!) and duly
threw it into an orange tree… and ran (somehow keeping
towel around me the whole time). Okay… that was fun.

Next we all called and sang HAPPY BIRTHDAY to Tippi.
I think she was really thrilled (all = auntie Lynn, two
nephews, and mom). Tippi giggled lots LOL. >>>

Oh yes, Chelsea was exhibiting some unusual behaviours and our trusty Doggie Doc decided it would be prudent to examine young pooch, including getting a urine sample. Oh… that was gonna be fun. The boys just couldn't wait to watch Auntie Lynn running around the garden after Chelsea with a wee bucket attempting to capture her output. Perhaps extreme detail is neither warranted or required on this occasion, but suffice to say said wee was captured, analysed, and Miss Pooch is just fine and dandy – jolly hockey sticks :o))))

Yesterday's ice-skating was all good… except for Josh being, well, Josh. As you well know he is incapable of doing anything (including sleeping) without thinking up some mischief, and in this case it was to skate up some ice to put in Lilia's hair. Olga's daughter flashed the eyes of her Russian Jewish Israeli Gypsy heritage and said, "He'll pay for that!" And so plans were made…

Lilia was invited for a sleepover last night. We waited until we THOUGHT both boys were asleep and sneaked into Josh's room and filled one hand with foaming soap. The crafty little urchin didn't move a muscle until we were almost out of the door again,
THEN……………………………………………

"'Allo," he grinned, mimicking Nicolas Cage's accent from National Treasure when he was in Buckingham Palace .
"You girls are in trouble!" Oh…………. Cr**……………

Lilia and I bolted (Lachlan slept like a stone all through this, by the way) but that didn't help us escape a good soaping. Grandma (naturally) wanted to know what all the commotion was about, so I reluctantly took full responsibility. I believe I have now been grounded from Joshua's 10th birthday party LOL.

Lilia came to try and take some of the heat off me   >>>

but when she returned to bed she suddenly SCREAMED because Josh had been waiting under her covers to ambush her (just as well he's only nine years old, hey??!!) (Lachlan slept through all this too!) Oh yes…

Did I mention earlier in the night all the kids decided it would be good fun to try on grandma's and Auntie Lynn's assorted wigs. You will find sample photographs below… some are absolute classics!!!!!!!!!! (I've put a couple of the ice-skating photos in ahead of the wig photos). BUT WAIT… THERE'S MORE…………….

Not to miss "the last word" this morning as I was sitting chained to my dungeon checking emails, Lilia charged into my office (astounding in itself as she would normally sleep through a hurricane up to lunchtime – amazing what motivation does) wanting to borrow a lipstick… not for her lips you understand. While Joshua really was still soundly in the land of nod this time, and with Lachlan's enthusiastic assistance (as Lachlan is always bright-eyed early in the morning) the two of them (Lilia and Lachlan) got quite creative with my best Dior red, and then took photos (a sample below). Josh later got up and had breakfast without an inkling. Then he found out… I think we're in trouble!!!!!!!!!!

Off to Cousin Laurence and the sub-cousins shortly. Mom is very afraid… six Santer men (Lachlan , Joshua, Cousin Laurence, and the three sub cousins) the worst of all – a Santer girl (me)… and Mom… she's looking for body armour LOL

Luff & hugz and pix follow

Sis xxxxxxxxxxxxxxxxxxxxxxxxxxxxxxxx

OLGA TEACHES JOSH TO SKATE ON ONE LEG

SLAVE LABOUR

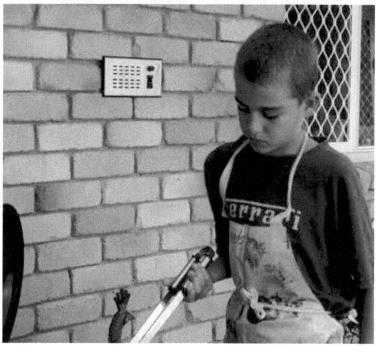

LILIA'S AND LACHLAN 'S ATTEMPTS AT FACE PAINTING SLEEPING JOSH BELOW

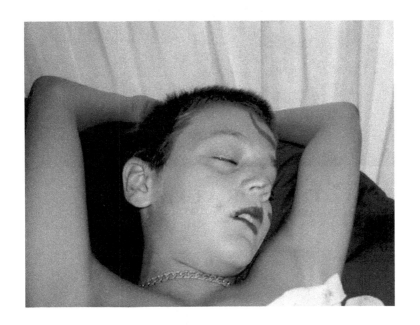

OKAY – YOU KNEW YOUR BOYS WERE BLONDES… RIGHT???!!!

HOWZ THIS FOR A CLASSIC SHOT?????????

I can see you having a real good belly laugh over this.
A very pissed off Auntie Lynn xxxxxxxxxxx

Aw… common… it's all a joke really. I AM still supposed to be able to get out them. Right? RIGHT??!!! **!&!^&!#& &*#!!!!

Excuse me? What do you mean… NO? I'm stuck in these things?? What the???? I thought we were a team! WHAT? GRANDMA GAVE YOU PERMISSION? DID I HEAR THAT RIGHT? (Check grandma's expression in the background!!!!)…………

AND VERY WORST OF ALL… HOW THE HECK AM I SUPPOSED TO DRINK MY WINE ALL CHAINED UP? I MEAN – GET REAL – GET SERIOUS – GET YOUR PRIORITIES STRAIGHT HERE… I MEAN IF I CAN'T DRINK MY WINE… OH… WAIT A MINUTE………………

Hey! I can drink my wine! Maybe it's not so bad…

Although… I have to say… THAT ENTIRELY ISN'T THE POINT…………… I TRUSTED YOU!!!!!

(And imagine grandma killing herself laughing in the background!!!)

And that, ladies and gentlemen, is the story of the first man who ever got me in chains... and it took a 12 year old to do it!!!! And do you know what the chicken shit had the NERVE to say to me afterwards? And I quote (as though this is gonna save him... HA... NOT!!!!) He said, "I only did it because you're my favourite aunt – playing tricks is the best way to keep a healthy relationship." NOW IT'S WAR!!!!!!!!!!!!!!

When Guy Thomas saw "Joshua's chain trick" he said he could see the headlines in the women's magazines now:

She's worked with celebrities...
She's trekked through jungles...
She's tracked wild predators on foot............
and brought down by a 12 year old!!!!!!!

MORE ON JOSHUA...
From his mother (my sister) 8th April, 2011

When I got up yesterday, there was a message on the kitchen bench from Josh (they are on school hols at the moment).

It went like this:

Hi Mum

I am meeting Liam at Casuarina to go to the movies at 9.15. I know I am really cute when I am asleep but can you PLEASE WAKE ME UP. Please leave me some money and do you know where the key to my safe is? Luv you Mummy. Josh :)

The gall of him hey!! This one is going in the archives for his 21st!

EVEN MORE ON JOSHUA

From: Lynn Santer
Subject: Amazing birthday

It was an amazing birthday yesterday starting with all sorts of calls, SMS, emails and gifties, but perhaps the most amazing call of all was from none other than our favourite former personal pilot for Saddam Hussein, Captain Ali Al Wahabi… all the way from Abu Dhabi!!!! He's doing well in his new post and is listing mom and I in his family and friends package for pilot's rates flights!!! I don't know that we'll be flying an Arab Emirates airline any time soon, but still it was very nice. He says he will be here in September and hopes to catch up with you then, so our "Passion for Peace" is still alive and well… isn't that wonderful?!

Among other calls yesterday morning were my little nephews. Young Joshua asked what I was doing for my birthday. I answered thus:

Olga for dinner – champagne

Friend (Deidre) arriving from Melbourne in the evening– champagne

Friend arriving from Brisbane tomorrow afternoon – champagne

Tomorrow night at Sheraton – lots of champagne

House guests to beach breakfast Sunday morning – hair of the dog champagne.
Josh thought for a moment and said, "Auntie Lynn, that's a very very very very very very very very very very very very very lot of champagne!"

Don't you love kids ??????????????

Merry Mayhem on the farm

Email to Tippi dated May 3rd, 2003, from my sister's farm in country Victoria (just outside Melbourne) when my nephews, Lachlan and Joshua, were around six and seven years old…

Did I say it would be merry mayhem if Auntie Lynn was left in charge of two little boys on the farm for a day? Well…

After we'd exhausted all the relatively "normal" channels of entertainment, it felt like a walk to the dam might be good exercise. This was quickly followed by a sojourn to the partially constructed lake – basically a mud pool. You can guess what's coming, can't you? Who needs to go to a beauty salon for a mud bath?

It started with races, but all too soon it degenerated into slipping and sliding and mud pie fights. I don't think there was an inch of them that wasn't covered in mud. So much for the nice clean clothes their mother left them in!!

The dogs naturally got in on the act… I won't even go there. Then (of course) it started raining! And it is NOT a quick walk to the house!

Honestly there wasn't a portion of Lachlan and Joshua not dripping in gooey mud – all exposed skin, every fibre of their clothing, and all throughout their hair. Apparently this is quite hilarious if you are a little boy.

The rules back at the house were: Strip off, leave everything outside, wash your hands in the laundry (which mercifully was right at the back door) then I would get some towels and they could shower and put clean clothes on (there was a shower right by the laundry too). >>>

"But you can't see us naked, Auntie Lynn," they complained.

"Trust me, I've seen bigger," I quipped back without thinking how much curiosity this would raise.

"Oh?" Lachlan mused. "Have you seen dad?"

"Er… NO!"

"Uncle Peter?"

"Er… NO!"

"Well who then?"

Gee, you can't say anything to a kid, can you?

Shortly thereafter my brother-in-law, Stephen, called from New York (where he was on business). The above conversation was recounted in full. I do believe it made his day!!!

Did I mention what the laundry and shower looked like afterwards? Jeepers, it was a mission to try and magically make everything look like nothing had happened before mom got home.

"Hey, Auntie Lynn," they called to me, as I was checking my manicure. "That was fun! Can we do it again?"

The pit in the grounds destined to become a lake wasn't deep enough to contain the depths my jaw fell to!! Again??!!!! I do NOT think so!!!!! So… how was I going to distract the little darlings next? >>>

I quickly decided on what I considered to be a safe option… dancing to Ricky Martin music, which we all enjoyed. Unfortunately the HiFi is in the formal lounge and apparently dancing has to be conducted on the formal furniture (like, everyone knows that, don't they?)

"Mum will freak out if she hears about this," I commented.

"So… we won't tell her," they smartly replied.

Okay, that sounded like a plan I could work with, but I nonetheless suggested dancing on the floor might be a preferred method. Oh my, you should have seen the two of them tangoing together – it was just hilarious. Then Josh insisted on tangoing with me.

Oh, and now there's a new addiction to "The Devil Went Down to Georgia" as the boys insisted over and over, "Sing it again, Auntie Lynn!"

I'm just off to renew my prescription for birth control pills!!!

Much love,
Auntie Lynn ☺ xxxxx

Moments to make you stop and think

Moving moment

I am sharing this because I called one friend today to tell her of this experience and she said to me, "You have no idea how much I needed to hear that right now, it has really helped me." So, if it helps one other person, that will be wonderful.

Today is Holocaust Remembrance Day. I am in no way a religious Jew, but I am nonetheless a Jew, and out of respect I attended a remembrance service put on by my wonderful Rabbi, Nir Gurevitch. Two things stand out for me.

One of the recordings played at this occasion was something discovered in the archives of The Smithsonian Institute. It was a BBC (UK) recording of the day the concentration camp, Belson, was liberated. Thousands of dead bodies lay around, not yet burned in the fires. More were dying even as the recording was being made.

Those who were being liberated had been physically and mentally tortured beyond our ability to comprehend. They were little more than skin on bone. Against this backdrop, to send a message to humanity, to send a message of the courage of the human spirit, and to say that goodness can NEVER be destroyed by evil, the survivors formed a choir and sang Hatikvah – the national anthem of the Jewish people.

The power, the sheer POWER of those voices was startling past my ability to adequately describe. Aside from the astonishing power in the voices of people who by all rights should be dead, every single one of them was singing in tune!!!

It was the single most amazing and inspirational thing I have ever heard in my life. And it reminded me >>>

of something that I told my friend of while I was recounting this story to her, that might in turn be helpful to someone else out there…

Another inmate of a concentration camp, Viktor Frankl, saw his family murdered before his eyes, and survived the Holocaust while writing a book inside his head. That book has subsequently been published and never – ever – gone out of print. It is called "Man's Search for Meaning". To boil down the entire book into a single sentence, Viktor said the following. But before I tell you that, put this into perspective. I think you will all have to accept whatever bad things may happen to you in your life, any illness that may befall you, any loved one you may lose, and business venture that goes sour, nothing – NOTHING that happens to you could possibly be as horrific, as horrendous, as heinous as being an inmate of a concentration camp. From that viewpoint, consider Viktor Frankl's words. There are some things you will never have control over in your life, no matter what you do, no matter what you believe in, no matter how much of a best seller things like "The Secret" or other variations dominate the best seller lists, BUT, **there is one thing you will NEVER lose control over, and that is your ability to choose how you react to any given situation.**

If this helps one other person out there I will be absolutely delighted.

And to prove we're not all over-poweringly profound and philosophical on this day, afterwards my gorgeous mother went up and chatted to the Rabbi – naturally. One of the points the Rabbi had made during the ceremony was no matter what we believe, or observe, or whatever, in a Rabbis eyes anyone born a Jew is a Jew regardless of anything else. This Rabbi knows precisely where my mother and I stand religious, or irreligious-wise. >>>

Anyway, mom, proud of me as she is, told the Rabbi that I will be attending the RSPCA's gala this Friday night. Embarrassed I jumped in and said, "Don't tell the Rabbi that, it's Friday night," – the evening of the Sabbath. However - in the Kabbalah, ancient Jewish mysticism, it tells us we are not masters of the planet but rather custodians of it, and the wildlife who share our lands are treated with great reverence. So, despite the fact that this event is on Friday night, the Rabbi's instinctive response to my mother was, "It's all right, I won't tell anyone." I just can't tell you the respect and admiration I have for this very special and truly very Holy man, in the most ancient and sincere respects of what those words mean.

Have a beautiful evening.

With love to all,
Lynn

Up in smoke… Smokers ARE people too!!!

Mom says she's heard that the Govt is considering charging people who need medical/hospital attention a "smoking premium" if their condition is smoking related. This is, apparently, quite separate from the proposed increase in the price on a packet of cigarettes, to pay for health care improvements. I can't find anything about this anywhere. Have you heard, or can you find out, anything about it? Whether we are smokers, reformed smokers, or non-smokers, if such a proposal is really being considered I believe it is not only fraught with danger and potential abuse, but it is outrageous, unconstitutional, unethical, and immoral, but of course smokers have no voice whatsoever to complain, which is equally outrageous so long as smoking is still a legal practice. Below I have listed some of the reasons I feel this way, which I am certain you can (please) add to. If you can find out if this is being considered, and if so who is considering it, no matter what anyone thinks about smokers, I believe my concerns below are valid and vital and should be addressed. Comments?

Hugz,

Sis ☺ xxxxxxxxxxxxx

1. Why charge smokers extra for medical care and not illicit drug users, when drug use is illegal while smoking is legal? (My guess would be because drug users never have any spare money, whereas smokers do!)
2. If we set the precedent for charging more for "self-inflicted" wounds, where does it end? Can we charge the morbidly obese for being glutens? Can we charge those with skin cancer for sitting in the sun? Where does the line get drawn once a legal precedent is in place? >>>

3.   Do we charge people in their 80s and 90s for smoking related conditions when they would have started smoking before anyone knew about the medical risks?

4.   What about reformed smokers? How long does one need to have stopped smoking before they are not charged a premium? A week? A month? A year? Ten years? And once this is decided, how is it proven?

5.   How can it be constitutional to charge smokers such a heavy premium in tax per packet of cigarettes to help fund a health policy, and then also charge them extra for smoking related illnesses? If they had all stopped smoking you would not have been able to fund your policies, so how is it fair and reasonable to then charge them extra when they get sick, when if they hadn't smoked you wouldn't have been able to raise the necessary funds for your programs? If a private company suggested such a policy wouldn't they be jailed for double dipping?

6.   What about people who are suffering smoking related conditions from passive smoking? How will you prove this wasn't "their fault", or will they be slugged the same premium for health care that actual smokers will because regardless they still have a smoking related condition?

7.   How do we ensure the system isn't abused when an individual may be deemed non-functional, or non-contributing to society they can easily be labelled as a smoker, or ex-smoker within whatever timeframe is established, and tossed out on the street to die an agonising death if they can't afford to pay the extra "smoking-related-condition" premium? >>>

From: Karen O'Brien
Sent: Friday, 16 April 2010 8:12 AM
To: Lynn Santer
Subject: Re: Smoking charges

Haven't heard will look into it. U should have been a
lawyer u fight a very good case!! U still off them?

***

Ha! Well, really – don't you think every point I put forward
is a valid one??? It makes my blood boil! Smokers are the
only segment of society I know who are penalised for doing
something completely legal, and until they make it illegal it
just isn't right, and it is a hundred times more not right that
as law-abiding, tax-paying, legitimate and valuable
members of society (both in their professions and in what
they pay in taxes on smokes) that they have no
constitutional voice – at all!!! It is WRONG!!!

That's to say nothing of people who contract lung cancer
who have NEVER smoked (and there's a surprisingly high
number of those) who are then treated like lepers because it
is automatically assumed by everyone that if they have lung
cancer they MUST be a smoker and therefore it's THEIR
fault and they deserve no sympathy or support! Wrong,
wrong, WRONG!!!!

'We've been disenfranchised!'

Hi Sandy,

I'm holding this year's Magical Scarecrows LET'S MAKE MAGIC FOR A DAY event for disabled and disadvantaged children with the RSPCA this year, which is fabulous because it brings Magical Scarecrows back where they really belong, into the world where we are caring for all creatures great and small. Of course they have been dubbed a children's project, because the stories are for children and the philanthropic programs benefit children, but the stories themselves were always designed to pass on my love of wildlife and respect for all animals to the next generation, so to me they were really always about animals.

This year the children from the charities I support (The Leukaemia Foundation, Camp Quality – which is kids with cancer, and Paradise Kids – which is kids in crisis that could be ill, abandoned, abused, etc) have all written stories about their favourite animals and drawn pictures of them. Those stories and pictures have formed the basis of a new special edition Magical Scarecrows book that I have donated to the RSPCA. This is thrilling in so many ways…

First, I have always wanted a way to publish stories written by children, ever since I sent my first Magical Scarecrows story to a publisher when I was only a child myself. The children are, of course, thrilled to see their work in print.

Second, it teaches children to think and write creatively, but more importantly than this, it also teaches them that no matter what their hardship or ailment they are still able to achieve something that positively contributes to society/the world.

The RSPCA are, of course, thrilled to have something quite unique to sell to raise money – so it really works for absolutely everybody. However, on a sadder note, of course the nature of these kids is such that some of them >>>

aren't going to make it. Normally I am emotionally removed from that side of it, but this year it was brought crashingly home to me with a name, a face, and a personality.

One of the little girls, only eight years old, who supplied one of the stories for the book, isn't going to make it to the event – she has entered the final stage of her illness and been admitted to hospital and will not be coming out. That is tragic of course, but why was I advised? Because the child's dying wish was to see her work in print, a wish I was of course only too happy to grant, along with sending a big pack of other Magical Scarecrows goodies.

At first my feelings were all over the place about this news, but when I thought about it I thought, you know what, (a) I have been able to grant the dying wish of a child – how amazing is that, and (b) because of my Magical Scarecrows this child is going to know something she has done will live on forever and will forever be something that is going to help animals... AND HOW AMAZING IS THAT????

As the philosopher Ralph Waldo Emerson said, "To know one life has breathed easier because you have lived, this is to have succeeded". Well, this little girl, at eight years old, will know that and I think this is, well, magic.

Good things always,
       The Kangaroo Kid... aka Auntie Lynn

Journals of the journeys

**Tanna girl proudly clings to her
Magical Scarecrows book**

IT'S NOT WHAT YOU GATHER,

BUT WHAT YOU SCATTER

THAT TELLS WHAT KIND OF LIFE YOU HAVE LIVED...

Extract from my biography "An Unbelievable Life" by Sandra L. Rogers, available from Zeus Publications...

You think you've seen a volcano erupt
– think again!

In December 1994, as everyone was gearing up for Christmas, Lynn was preparing to return to Australia for her sister's wedding. Neville (Lynn's father) had flown Continental Airlines much of his business life, and as a result had millions of frequent flyer points. Once Continental no longer flew to Australia, Neville gifted the points to Lynn. With those she bought a first class London – Los Angeles return ticket and then with cash bought an economy class United Airlines LA – Melbourne ticket as she had an upgrade certificate to business class from her win at the AmCham competition.

Very excited about her sister's wedding, she checked her bags in at London Airport through to Australia and off she went! London to LA transited in New York and this was during the Thanksgiving holiday when all was pandemonium. Soon she discovered her flight to LA had been delayed by three hours and with her transit time in LA only three hours this would make the follow on connection to Australia impossible. She duly marched off to Continental and explained her situation, where her sister was getting married and that this would be a very tight squeeze to say the least, probably not going to make it. Actually Karen was due to marry Stephen in one week's time but Lynn desperately told them the wedding was tomorrow! As you would!

They told her not to worry as there was another flight leaving soon for LA and they would get her on that one.

When she arrived at that counter, they said: "It's over booked but don't worry, your original flight will be leaving sooner than expected so go back to your original flight and all will be okay."

Off she trundled back to her original flight, boarded the aircraft and stayed sat there until it took off two hours and forty five minutes later. "Am I having fun yet?" she whispered under her breath.

Calling the in-flight staff over she explained what had happened … again! They reassured her saying they would call ahead and make sure her luggage would be the first off the plane, and the staff would take her directly to her United flight.

So she sat back and relaxed until she landed in LA and none of that happened! Instead she arrived at the United gate just in time to see her plane in the sky!

Be assured at that point Mount Vesuvius had nothing on an erupting Lynn!

She stormed off to the nearest Continental desk, where there was a long line of people waiting. Naturally she ignored the line, pushed to the front and growled, "Get your manager here. Now!!"

The girl behind the desk saw the blaze of a lion in the eyes before her. She didn't even ask Lynn why, she just got on the loudspeaker and called the manager over.

The manager duly arrived and Lynn looked him in the eye saying, "I apologise in advance for everything I'm about to say to you, because I know this is none of your fault personally, but it's Continental's mess and YOU are going to clean it up!" Ever the actress, by now Lynn was saying that Karen's wedding would be completely missed!

So he said, "Let's see when the next flight to Australia is."

The next flight of any sort was the next morning on a Qantas flight and he told Lynn that he could transfer the economy ticket but not the upgrade."

To that Lynn replied, "I don't think so! This is YOUR mess and you are going to clean it up. I will not be flying cabbage class because of something you've done."

When he replied there was nothing he could do about it because there was no one with a higher authority, Lynn snapped.

"Really? Are you the president of Continental Airlines?" His answer was No. "Well then, there is someone with a higher authority, isn't there? And I suggest you get him to speak to me, or…"

Knowing he could not win with this fiery vixen he asked her where she was staying and promised he'd get someone to call her. "NO!" she spat. "YOU tell me where I'm staying, and have them call me."

"Of course. We'll organise accommodation for you."

He did and he gave her food vouchers. Naturally Lynn ordered every expensive dish on the menu. She didn't eat anything, as she was far too upset, and needless to say she didn't sleep. This gave her all night to write the 'speech'… several times.

When the general manager of Continental Airlines phoned her the next morning he mumbled again about not being able to transfer the upgrade certificate.

"Really?" Lynn rumbled. "What else have you been told?"

"Nothing. Just that you are travelling on an economy ticket with an upgrade certificate and we can't transfer the upgrade certificate."

He then received the 'speech'! By this version of the speech Karen was pregnant!

After that he said, "Give me five minutes."

She checked her watch. He called her back in three.

"Right," he said. "Go to Qantas first class ticketing. Don't queue, they are expecting you."

Off she went to Qantas, heard an Australian accent, and burst into tears, "You won't believe what these terrible Americans have done to me!"

They deftly gave her a box of tissues and checked her into first class rather than business.

Note to self: remember to cry when checking in at an airline counter!

So there she is finally sitting in her first class seat on her way to Australia when she realised she hadn't seen her suitcases since London. I wonder where they are. She called the in-flight staff over and told them the whole long story all over again; and by now of course Karen was getting a divorce!

The Qantas staff assured her they would look into it.

Finally at Melbourne Airport there was a loud announcement for Miss Santer.

"What now?" she wondered exhaustedly, dragging one foot in front of the other to where she had been summoned.

"Are you Miss Santer?"

"Yes."

With steely eyes the staff member said, "Do you see the exit of the airport down there? Well your suitcases are there. Please take them and GO!"

Note to self: if you make a nuisance of yourself it just might help, although probably not today with all the security measures in place.

Lynn carrying her sister's train.

Lynn and her father Neville at Karen and Stephen's wedding

Another extract from my biography "An Unbelievable Life" by Sandra L. Rogers, available from Zeus Publications...

The birth of my first nephew, Lachlan

Before the baby was born, Lynn had told Karen that she couldn't be there for the birth as she would be at a conference in Spain. In fact Lynn had made a promise to herself there would be no other place on earth she would be but beside her sister when her first child was born. Neville and Clare knew this but Karen and Stephen did not. As it turned out an Oracle conference in Kuala Lumpur popped up just before the baby was due, which was perfect timing and location. This also enabled Lynn to get a tax deduction for the trip.

Prior to the Oracle conference in KL, Lynn had been trying for months to secure a meeting with one Brian Hall, who was then the managing director of Royal & Sun Alliance in the UK, a man she wanted involved in her negotiations for the new pensions' legislation. After much angst a meeting had finally been secured a few days prior to her planned trip to KL and onto Australia. It all seemed very neatly organised. I said it "seemed" that way...

The day before her meeting with Brian, Clare called from Australia.

"If you want to be here for the birth of this baby you had better drop everything and come immediately."

There had been some complications and if not rectified by Friday the baby would have to be induced. Lynn thought, 'Bugger! I'll have to go straight to Australia and miss the conference ... and the tax deduction!' Let's get one's priorities in order here! Then the dilemma came as to whether she should reschedule the meeting she'd fought so hard to secure with Brian Hall, or risk delaying her trip by 24 hours, which should still get her to Australia prior to Friday. She opted to keep the meeting. Turning up at the assigned time and place she waited … and waited … and waited. Mr Hall stood her up. Oh boy was she wild!

Never one to mince her words Lynn wrote Brian the most stinking email you can imagine, not caring that he was one of the most important men in the initiative. She had put off a flight to Australia – for the birth of her sister's first child – for this man, and he didn't show … he didn't even call to apologise. She wasn't taking any prisoners, she wasn't accepting surrender, she went straight to execution!

Later Lynn was to learn that when this serious heavy weight in the business blinkingly read her email a slow smile crept across his lips. He sent her a reply which went something like this: "What would kill most people doesn't even embarrass me. In fact I choose to deal with people who are straight talkers, which you clearly are, so when you get back to London I would like to meet you for a cup of tea." As it turned out he'd had a terrible flu and that was why he had stood her up. From then on Brian became one of Lynn's biggest supporters. He would love to dine out and tell people about the email she had sent him, "Ask me what Lynn said without the swear words … nothing!" In years to come Brian was to ironically play a pivotal role in Karen's life. Karen and Stephen were running a baby animal farm at the time, and had public liability insurance with HIH when they went bust overnight. Karen returned home that day to discover a letter that said if they didn't take out new insurance (having only just paid a year's premium the month before) with a new company at FOUR TIMES the premium by close of business that day they would not be insured. If they were not insured they would be out of business. It was already 4 p.m., no alternative companies were immediately offering this kind of insurance, and they couldn't afford to pay four times the premium they had already paid only one month before. Karen called Lynn in a panic. While it was after business hours in Australia, the business day was only just starting in London and guess who came to the rescue … Brian Hall!

Having to leave London earlier than planned to be in Australia for the birth of her sister's first child, Lynn had to come up with an excuse as to why she wouldn't be in her London home should Karen call with any news. Accordingly she told Karen that she was leaving earlier than planned for Spain to attend some meeting or another, and would call from there to see how things were going. Lynn assumed she could use the phone on the plane to regularly check in, but as it turned out the satellite link was out the whole way. When she stopped in Dubai she raced off the plane, checking what time it would be in Spain and rang Karen pretending she was having breakfast in Spain. She raced off the plane again at the next stopover in KL and did the same thing. Finally in Melbourne the man in customs asked, "Have you anything to declare?" and she told him, "Yes! I'm about to become an aunt!" They hurried her through. She raced to the taxi and went straight to the hospital.

Note to self: Always tell customs' agents you are about to become an aunt!

On seeing her frantic sister running through the hospital door Karen's eyes nearly popped out of her head. The first words out of her shocked mouth were, "Spain! I'm never going to believe you again!" And she nearly popped the kid out right there on the spot!

Being very pragmatic, as Lynn was, she said, "Look, here's the situation. I really was supposed to be at a conference in KL first and there's a huge tax deduction at stake here, so if you could please be induced in short order I can still turn around, make the conference and come back to have the originally-planned two weeks here with you." Karen, bless her little heart, went to her gynaecologist and explained, making Lynn's request. Can you believe it? By return Lynn's sweet sister was told in no uncertain terms, "I'm sorry dear, but your sister's tax deduction is not a primary consideration here!"

So Lynn went home and unpacked her Melbourne things, re-packed her KL things, booked every flight out of Melbourne to KL until it would have been too late, went back to the hospital with her packed case, and paced. On day two she found herself out on the smoking balcony, lit a cigarette, had a few puffs, and only then realised she wasn't alone. Out of the corner of her eye she noticed Stephen standing there as pale as a ghost and shaking so badly he couldn't get a cigarette in his mouth. He was completely incapable of speaking.

"Stephen? Are you okay? Is there any news?"

Lachlan had been born but not without some drama. At one point it had even been touch and go there for a while, but finally nephew number one had arrived with all his fingers and toes, healthy and well, into the world shared by his lunatic aunt. Shortly thereafter they were introduced for the first time.

Looking down at his little cherub face Lynn tried not to cry with joy. No, that would never do. She had a reputation of being a tough bitch, she wasn't going to cry! Instead she turned and said to the baby, "There are certain things you need to know. First, welcome to the world, I'm your aunt. Second, diamonds are good. Third, I've gotta go to KL and get a tax deduction now!" And off she went.

That initial training was to prove successful as on his first flight, before he could talk, Lachlan had learned to point and say, "Ta?" when he wanted something. Wobbling up and down the aisles of the plane he spotted a lady wearing a huge diamond ring. He pointed to it and said, "Ta?" The husband smiled at Karen and told her that her son had good taste. Karen could only shake her head, knowing where that came from. When she told Lynn what had happened the powerhouse aunt grinned, "Oh, I'm so proud!"

From: Lynn Santer
Subject: Trip to Vanuatu
Date: Sun, 31 May 2009 08:52:28

Yes – I signed a deal!!! A FILM DEAL!!! I'll explain as
the story unfolds…

To begin at the beginning… I landed at Port Vila airport to
beautiful balmy breezes and a Polynesian band soothing the
savaged travellers. Seeing the pristine blue skies was
welcome relief too because right up until the night before
there had been tropical storms of fearsome magnitude for
the past week. I just love it when the sun shines for me!!

After completing the obligatory new swine flu
questionnaire I made it through customs with all the
contraband that Paul had asked me to bring to the island
without incident and he spotted me immediately, which
isn't a bad effort for someone who's never met me before
and only seen photos of me as a brunette!

Much as Alain once did in Paris, instead of taking me home
to settle in, I was whisked directly from the airport to take
in some of the local sights. In Paris I only remembered
hours later that I had caviar in my luggage and the sun was
beating down cooking it in the trunk – ouch! In this case,
however, I think the contraband was going to survive the
heat (no caviar).

Initially I was taken to the local fruit and veggie market,
where locals were sitting on the dirt floor in raggedy
clothes chatting casually among themselves surrounded by
their produce as we meandered around deciding what we'd
like. I didn't stick out much (cough!!) wearing jet black
and hot pink, dripping in designer everything and
diamonds!! Oh dear!!

Then it was off to the "civilized" supermarket to see what delicacies I might be in need of there, which was rather amusing as it became evident that Paul usually has his local staff do the shopping so he didn't know his way around the supermarket that well, but for a Hollywood film producer who only resides in this third-world tropical paradise for two months a year he managed pretty well. The only thing then left to procure was eggs, which I was advised one does not purchase at the supermarket, there's a special "eggery" to attend for that. Ha! Standard sizes were clearly something they'd never heard of. These eggs came in all sizes, some so big I think they must have been laid by ostriches! And trying to put them into a standard carton was a bit moot… there was no way the carton was going to shut so I had to keep it on my lap from then on.

At "Paul's palace" with sweeping vistas of the South Pacific Ocean, tropical foliage, and villages below, we were greeted by Phoebe and Lola, the two hounds, with "smiles" – honestly – these dogs smile (everyone on Vanuatu smiles… even my cell phone turned on with the message… You're in Vanuatu – SMILE… really!!!)

As we sat on the balcony, a hound on each side, while Anne-Marie (the house keeper) served us drinks, I learned that Paul has a string of famous credits under his belt, both on TV and in film, including (to name but a few) "MacMillan and Wife", "Ironside", "CHIPS", oh don't get me started, it's a REALLY long list. Another American Ex Pat wandered in while we were chatting, Ken, and he was duly invited with his wife for dinner the following night.

After unpacking it was Martini hour, and some of the contraband I'd procured was put to good use – only the finest vodka and let me tell you that Paul knows how to make one mean martini… naturally shaken not stirred. ☺ We supped and chatted further as Mother Nature turned on a spectacular sunset for us – utterly breathtaking. Only once the sun was safely nestled away for the night did we venture out for dinner to a beach front restaurant just down the road, which again was utterly breathtaking (this gets monotonous after a while, doesn't it? LOL).

I heard the story of how "Hachiko" was made (his current film with Richard Gere that premieres in Japan 8th July and should be here in October). I lost count of how many rewrites the script went through – a lot! He kept wanting to show it to me but having not even survived the You Tube clips without blubbering uncontrollably I wouldn't allow it. This is one MAJOR weepy film… and a true story.

We also discussed a new perfume business he's getting into. There's a plant on the island with an extremely romantic and exotic legend surrounding it, reputed to be an aphrodisiac if worn by men or women, and coming from French Vanuatu in the South Pacific you can imagine the marketing spin potential. He's quite a way along the development path of this new line so we chatted about which celebrities I know who might be appropriate to become the "face" of this new product when it's launched. As the process to produce it necessarily involves separating the components of the plant my mind naturally drifted to Cousin Laurence's bio fuel processors, especially as one of the bi-products from perfume plant production is oil, which is what Cousin Laurence turns into diesel and electricity on third world islands such as Tonga, Samoa, Fiji, PNG, etc - so now Paul and Cousin Laurence are chatting too ☺

Returning to my guest bungalow on the property that night I was greeted by a massive and beautiful black and white moth, which I was duly polite to before resting my head for a peaceful night's sleep.

Incidentally, it didn't take me long to establish that Paul Mason was originally Paul Bloomberg, a Russian Jew – ah we get everywhere, don't we?

As the sun lazily rose its dazzling head over another glorious day in paradise I was greeted leaving my bungalow by the smiling hounds, keen for their morning constitutional. I have to say I struggled (a little) to keep up with this spritely almost eighty year old over the rugged terrain that "walkies" took us through, and smiled when we both had to chase after the dogs, who had inadvertently frightened the heck out of some passing natives. Puffed and sweaty I needed to bathe all over again before breakfast. Tropical song birds serenaded me in the shower as I tried to keep reminding myself I was there on business… business… remember business??!!

Entering the main house I discovered strains of Rogers and Hammerstein's "South Pacific" very appropriately playing as Anne-Marie (the house keeper) asked what I'd like her to prepare for my breakfast. I have to tell you – a girl could get used to this!!! As "Bali Hai" cheered out over our omelettes and croissant I soaked in the vistas of white sands and aqua waters, trying desperately to remember I was there TO PITCH. What the hell? There was time… I was gonna enjoy this!!!

After breakfast Paul took me to "The Secret Garden", a tucked away attraction displaying and explaining many of the myths, legends and history behind Vanuatu and its people, dating back to cannibalistic times. As part of the tour (for which we were the only tourists) we also met some of the native wildlife, namely an iguana, a python and a coconut crab. In sequence, the iguana was about a foot long, vivid green and calmly munching on a flower when I found him deposited on my shoulder. Like everything on the island, it was so relaxed it was unbelievable. Paul smiled and took the creature from me as we moved onto the next enclosure. While this wasn't the biggest python I've ever seen, it was also a long way from the smallest, I guess around seven or eight feet in length, and this time our guide wound it around my neck… several times. You know me,

I'm perfectly comfortable in the company of reptilian curly pals, but of course Paul does not know me and said, "MOST people would show at least SOME fear!" (TEE HEE!!!!) When I asked him if he'd like to hold my curly reptilian pal he politely declined, causing our native guide to smile broadly. Then it was onto the Coconut Crab. As relaxed as all three of these creatures were I drew the line there… you should have seen the size of this thing, and those pincers could have taken a finger off without skipping a heartbeat – no thanks – pass.

From there we chugged our way to the coast and took a ferry (tin boat) to Hide Away Island to go snorkelling with the fish… I REALLY HADN'T FORGOTTEN I WAS THERE TO PITCH… HONEST!!!!!

OMG!!! There were SO MANY fish, from tiny electric blue fish, to giant rainbow coloured fish, and just about everything you can imagine in between including striped angel fish feeding from glistening coral… I just have to say it was another of those monotonous utterly breathtaking moments, especially as Paul had brought food with and the fish eat right out of your hand – I was in heaven – and this was only a few feet out from the shore!!!! A few meters further out and I discovered the world's only underwater post office, now that was someone's ingenious idea. I only wish I'd known in advance so I could have brought a letter with to post – next time.

Of course I hadn't thought to bring any of my snorkel gear with me, I didn't even take a camera… I was there on business… remember… business? Fortunately Paul had spares for guests, and it was just as well because the island itself has stretches of razor sharp coral on the beach, which I looked at somewhat horrified having nothing resembling appropriate footwear with me. Paul just grinned and produced a pair of wet boots in exactly the right size… hummmmmmmm……

Over lunch on Hideaway Island I learned that some study or another has named Vanuatu "The Happiest Place on Earth" and I don't doubt it to be true... even their cemeteries look cheerful!!!

Waiting for the return "ferry" I spotted a bright orange shell in amongst the washed out coral and collected it like a child with a trophy, and sad person that I am I even brought it home with me. Well... I can be a kid if I want to! Oh wait... I was there on business... remember... business?????!!!!!!!!

When we returned to Paul's palace pitching just had to begin in earnest – but more on that later (I'm a tease, aren't I? LOL). It's far more important to tell you that the sunset that night was a perfect sphere of orange fireball – SPECTACULAR... as, once again, were the vodka martinis.

That night ex pat Ken and his wife Katie, together with my good friends Lindsay and Diana, came over for a dinner of Shabu Shabu, where more of my contraband was put to good use, this time the Sake, which is not available anywhere on Vanuatu. Over dinner Diana and I did some serious gossiping about "The A team"/Pest Control, discussing in earnest one of their recent divorces, as Diana told me all about this chap's new girlfriend in infinite detail. Only as Lindsay and Diana were getting in their car to go home did we realise we'd been talking about two entirely different members of the group. Paul and Lindsay looked at each other and burst out laughing at us!!!!!

Okay, you want to know about the business side of the trip, don't you? DON'T YOU? Well, the upshot of assorted pitching is as follows:

1.　　　　Paul has taken an entire collection of Magical Scarecrows merchandise to discuss retail potential with his son in the US!!! HOWZAT???? I told him the whole story, starting with the first approach to a publisher at nine years old, rewriting the stories for my nephews, and I showed him Lachlan and Joshua's written permission to share the stories in the front of the original books, along with their opening chapter illustrations. I also went through the whole T-Shirt saga, gave him a copy of that book, and showed him the DVD of the recent Dreamworld event. So, that's that.

2.　　　　We also discussed "Land of the Free" in some detail, and I showed him the documentary I'd had made on that as well. He's taken that one away to "marinate" over.

3.　　　　Next up was "The Edge of Reality", which most folks don't even know about. Turns out he has some awesome musical connections he plans to discuss this with in an attempt to package it up to the point where we can finally pitch it to Priscilla. Despite all my conversations with her I have never mentioned this project because I know it's not ready yet and Paul told me I'd done exactly the right thing there.

4.　　　　Then came "Sins of Life". This became very interesting as Sandy (Jack Nicholson's agent of 47 years and my good friend of 15 years) has recently told me he is actively looking for new projects for Jack. We sent Sandy an email and it turns out that Sandy remembers Paul well (as they've worked together before) and they've agreed to meet when Paul is back in LA to discuss the possibility of attaching Jack to the project!!!!!!!!! I had already sent "Sins of Life" to Sandy when he told me he was looking for a project, but of course no matter how good the project it's no good without a producer, so when I emailed Sandy from Paul's palace I told him I had one of those now... found one lurking around Vanuatu... LOL. Okay, so far that's Magical Scarecrows, Priscilla/Edge of Reality, Jack Nicholson/Sins of Life... am I doing okay so far???? BUT WAIT... THERE'S MORE.....

5.   I took with me a TON of material on just about every project I've ever been involved with or am about to be involved with to sift through seeing what might strike a chord... well... get ready for this... the one that REALLY grabbed him was... ALBY'S BIOGRAPHY! Oh no, I can hear everyone groaning already. I explained to Paul in no uncertain terms how Alby and I fought like cats and dogs over four years, and even entertained him with several Alby anecdotes, but he was not to be dissuaded... this was the one that particularly grabbed him. Is the world (or anyone in it) ready for another four years of Lynn and Alby????????????? Soooooooooooo.....

I called Alby after our dinner guests left from the privacy of my guest bungalow. After he'd finished choking that I was in Vanuatu staying with a Hollywood film producer (lolololololololololololololololololololol) he was all for the idea. Needless to say I couldn't wait for the next dawn.

Impatiently pacing the patio waiting for Paul to arise FINALLY I heard the click of the front door and he peered his head around announcing, "The office is open" (he'd

already worked out I get the shakes if I'm away from email for too long). There was no discussing business before breakfast (house rules) so I thought I might as well see what was on email. What was on email was an email from Channel Nine with a You Tube link to the story they've just aired on me… TALK ABOUT TIMING!!!!! Here's the link, and of course I called Paul in to watch it straight away… house rules be hanged!!!!!
http://www.youtube.com/watch?v=BB27ClEtcnM

He was duly impressed and asked me to email the link, which I did, adding, "While you're there, here's another link you might want…" and showed him Alby's You Tube. Again he was duly impressed at which point I casually added, "Well, I spoke to him last night." Paul looked up at me with an expression that said, "Of course you did." Anyway… AFTER BREAKFAST we had a Skype meeting with Alby, well… Skype… cell… we utilised all technology as between the connections in Vanuatu and the connections wherever Alby was… you can imagine. Nonetheless, we got the job done and Alby, bless his cotton sox, SANG MY PRAISES… even to the point of insisting a clause go into the agreement that said I was – at all times – to be involved in the project and if at any time I wasn't then he would withdraw his support!!!!!!!!!!! I stood there absolutely beaming, which Paul annoyingly informed Alby about, and when the meeting concluded (remembering I'd told Paul EXACTLY how the two of us had fought over, well, everything) Paul explained, "He trusts you… because he knows the devil you are!" HAHAHAHAHAHAHAHAHAHAHAHAHAHAHAHAHA.

IT GETS BETTER!!!!!!!!!!!!!!!!!!

Because Hugh Jackman has become such a fan of my Magical Scarecrows/T-Shirt project/s (to the point where his people PHONE ME) we are going to pitch the Alby story to Hugh!!!!!!!!!!! There are plans afoot for this I won't go into here but we're extremely hopeful about the prospects.

Following the virtual meeting Paul and I repaired to the balcony to draw up a Letter of Agreement between the three of us as the South Pacific Ocean lapped beneath us and gentle balmy breezes surrounded us, after which we decided a celebration was in order…

At Nambatu Lagoon, a place known largely only to locals, you'll find L' Chaumie restaurant, a divine thatched edifice with a pontoon over the lagoon where one can watch dozens of hungry fishes waiting patiently underfoot for patrons to drop a morsel or two (or in my case several). More palm trees, white sands, natives fishing across the lagoon with hounds at their sides, yes it was another of those monotonous utterly breathtaking moments replete with coconut prawns and champagne and once again we were the only patrons (the place is normally frequented for dinner).

After lunch I returned to the office (which has Paul's named director's chair and several film and TV awards around it) to type up the Agreement which Paul and I have now both signed and I have ready for Alby's paw print. ☺ We also decided it would be fun to send a joint postcard to Sandy from Vanuatu, so we did that too. ☺

The final evening began with drinks in Lindsay's office in town, before heading out to "The Calcutta" (a gambling event) which was hosted at a place called "The Saloon", an establishment owned by another ex pat Yank and designed to be a little piece of America in the South Pacific, complete with road signs (like in M*A*S*H) pointing to Los Angeles, San Fran, etc – very cool. There was a big raffle too… and guess who ended up drawing it – LOL… Vanuatu knew I was there. ☺

After a relaxing final morning it seemed I was not going to escape without at least seeing some of "Hachiko". Bracing myself, and calculating the shortest route to the nearest box of tissues, he showed me only a few excerpts of the film, and I have to say it is exquisitely made. I will watch it when it is released – behind dark glasses, with no make up, and a truck load of Kleenex!!

And yes, he'll look at other projects as they develop too.

Sadly the time came to depart. The Polynesian band was once again at the airport entertaining the intrepid travellers with melodic strains of Island songs as I gazed towards what can laughingly be called the departure board only to notice – with horror – that my flight wasn't listed. In a more familiar Western panic I inquired about this only to be told not to worry about it, they only show the flights they feel like!!!!!!! Gee this was reminding me of Africa!!!!!!!!!!!!!! At check in I beamed widely, blinked my big blue eyes innocently, and told the big black man behind the counter how much I loved his country. Displaying a huge row of pearly whites he asked me where I'd like to sit. "A window seat would be nice please, as near to the front as I can get it." "Well," he smiled back. "As you love Vanuatu so much I'll give you 2A." (Good-o – that worked ☺) I then asked what time we departed. The answer? A shrug, as in, "Who cares?" OY VEY. Was there a departure gate on my boarding card? Don't be silly!!! Did they check my liquids were in a plastic bag at customs? Please – that would be close to stress. But on the matter of stress…

With a harsh thump back to reality there was a bit of excitement on the aircraft – FOUR people in THE ROW BEHIND ME were taken off the plane at Brisbane in masks by authorities with suspected swine flu!!

Oh boy, you should have seen Chelsea when I returned. Somehow she knew even when the car was approaching the house and started barking like crazy. As I stepped through the front door she became a living pogo-stick at the gates to the entrance hall (bouncing up and down like a cartoon character) and for her next trick the moment after I greeted her she ran circles around the house at such velocity she became a blur!! She's eleven and a half years old! I think she was pleased to see me!

Mom told me she'd been moping in and out of my office looking for me and even when mom took out the special "blankie" we like to sit on together Chelsea would get on it for a moment, look at mom as if to say, "Don't be silly, it's no good on my own," and trudge off to her basket. She's happy now though, having slept all night under my covers and currently munching on a breakfast treat.

So ends my report.

Love always,
Auntie Lynn
☺
xxxxxxxxxxx

Yes, there really are three live snakes around my neck!!

ALBY, PORT VILA, AND TANNA, November, 2010

This has been THE most amazing week of my life, and if you know my life story that is saying quite something. Stay with me, you'll understand why as events gradually unfold… especially once we get to the Tanna part of the journey.

First off, not 24 hours before I left Australia I received a list of medical supplies that the "clinic" in Tanna was in desperate need of. I looked at this list in horror wondering how the hell I was going to pull that miracle off – at all – never mind with so little notice – especially when one of the items was a wheelchair for the local chief!!!! But never one to be defeated, I contacted "Dr Gorgeous" and he jolly well came through with the supplies – everything but the wheelchair which I ended up finding (and buying) from a supplier in Sydney and having FedExed over to Tanna (at twice the cost of the wheelchair itself I might add) but hey – mission accomplished – pretty cool start I thought. ☺

The trip began with me checking in at Brisbane airport before Alby arrived from Adelaide and booking the window seat. After doing the obligatory currency exchange and duty free shopping I went to the gate lounge and waited – and waited – no Alby. I called to see if he'd arrived in Brisbane – no answer. I called his sister Ria (known on Tanna as Maria for future reference) to check he'd left Adelaide okay. She went into instant panic. Then I spotted the guy who'd checked me in on boarding duties at the gate and asked him if my travelling companion had showed up. Rolling his eyes and sighing a little he confirmed that Alby had checked in and had apparently kicked up a hell of a fuss because he didn't have a window seat and had been duly allocated a window seat in the row behind me. So that was the start – because we both stubbornly refused to give up our favourite positions in the window we weren't even in the same row on the flight.

Alby eventually presented himself literally as the flight was boarding (naturally) asking innocently if I knew where we were sitting (as if he wouldn't know). Whatever. As it happened, as we were travelling at the front of the bus, we actually had three rows to ourselves so it was all entirely academic because I had upgraded us both.

Paul Mason had already been in Port Vila from Hollywood for a few days and was waiting for us at the airport on arrival. Having stayed for many months each year in his holiday home in Vila over the past six years he obviously knew the island, the people, the customs, etc backwards, and so en route back to his place when he saw two island girls needing a lift he stopped to pick them up. I was sitting in the front passenger seat of his 4WD, Alby was in the back... now with two island girls whom he instantly had in fits of giggles. Paul continued to attempt to talk to Alby until I reminded him who he was dealing with (after all Paul and I had spent the last 18 months working on the screenplay of Alby's life story so he should know the personality he was dealing with here). I pointed out: "Paul, if you think Alby can hear a word you're saying when there are two girls in the back with him – forget it – you're wasting your breath." Alby did manage to hear that comment clearly enough, apologised to Paul and gave him his full attention, which only served to produce a large smirk on Paul's face.

Of course as soon as we arrived at Paul's place, after the unavoidable "oos" and "ahs" at the property and the view, Alby was off for a run – in the midday sun. He just can't stay still for five seconds. Paul and I simply let him go while we opted for a more leisurely swim in the infinity pool overlooking a panoramic view of the island.

Dinner that night was with Paul's and my mutual friend, Lindsay Barrett, the number one accountant on Vanuatu, and boy did he lay on a spread for us. In his own palatial edifice, Lindsay had his staff prepare a full silver service spread on the expansive patio and the cheapest wine he served from a complete and apparently bottomless bar was Moet.

The next day was relatively relaxed waiting for Jenny and Andrew from New Idea magazine to arrive. Paul and I collected them while Alby was naturally running around the island again – and I do mean that quite literally. Of course Jenny and I go back many years, and have previously produced two Alby stories (once when she was still at Woman's Day and once after she'd moved to New Idea and we produced a come back story to Judy Green's outburst last year). Andrew was new to the picture and had no idea of the dynamics operating. He was just like a kid in a candy store. He was excited enough when he'd heard he had a job in Vanuatu, then more so when he discovered the Tanna element, then even more so when he learned part of that would be climbing an active volcano, but when he was finally told this was an Alby Mangels story he was quite incoherent with excitement as a huge fan of Alby's – and these were the first media to EVER travel with Alby so it's quite a coup for them.

There were no more spare rooms in Paul's place for Jenny and Andrew's one night on Vila before we moved to Tanna, so Paul had arranged for them to stay with very good friends of his on the island, Zvika and Outi. Paul and I took Jenny and Andrew straight there to settle in from the airport. Oh my goodness gracious me – it is hard to describe the full grandeur of Zvika and Outi's home. Let's start with the infinity pool almost right on the ocean is twenty-two meters long. It was quite breathtaking. Zvika spotted something in me the moment he laid eyes on me. "What's your background?" he asked in a rumbling Israeli accent reminiscent of Topol. "Russian Romanian…" I began to answer before he jumped back in saying, "I thought so. Shalom." I looked up and saw a Mezuzah on the front the door – not something I ever expected to see in Vila.

Jenny and Andrew settled in while I got to know Zvika's three dogs, including a boxer called Pablo who literally flies through the air, which he demonstrated to perfection with newly muddied paws that landed squarely on my brand new pristinely white trousers! Not happy Jan. ☹

Once settled, Jenny and Andrew were taken to Paul's place for the sunset tradition of martini sipping while Jenny had an opportunity to interview Paul about the Alby feature film. We passed Alby just returning home on approach to Paul's property so I opened the window and called out, "There goes the tone of the neighbourhood!" Andrew just couldn't wait to get his camera out and got some great shots of Alby jumping straight in the pool, and then of Paul, Alby and I together. Alby declined a martini this night (which he'd imbibed in the night prior) saying he'd rather share mine – cheek! Get your own – I want a whole one! But no.

Incidentally, there will be no photos until after the story is out because if ANYTHING gets out through other means prior to New Idea getting this story out then there will be no story. So we all have to be patient for photos (and there are some AWESOME ones – I haven't even got going yet). The story will likely not be in print prior to December some time.

Dinner that night was at Tamanu – a simply exquisite French restaurant right on the beach dripping with ambience… and what a fun night it was. Everyone was getting along with everyone so very well it was unbelievable. And Zvika completed the night by having everyone in stitches telling us the story of how he and Outi met. She was a Finnish nurse and he was convinced she would have nothing to do with an Israeli Jew so he told her that he was an Italian ski instructor instead. Regaling us with the entire saga that unfolded, dripping with charisma and charm in that richly intoxicating Israeli accent, he explained she organised their next date on a ski slope. Zvika had never put on a pair of snow skis in his life and ended up falling flat on his face. Anyway, long story short he won the heart and hand of his intended – it was a wonderful anecdote.

The next morning we were finally off to Tanna and our mission to help out bringing water and medical supplies to the villages. We had expected to be paying significant excess baggage costs as we were only allowed 10KG each. Andrew had that much in his hand luggage alone, and I was carrying two boxes of Magical Scarecrows books for the village children on top of my regular luggage. We had about 17 pieces between the four of us, much of which was Andrew's camera gear. We stood there holding our collective breaths as the very casual islander checked in bag – after bag – after bag – and then just waved us through! It was apparently all too hard to calculate how much excess baggage it really was so he just let us get away with it – very cool!! I then went to buy us all bottles of cold water and there wasn't enough change behind the counter so they offered me a lollipop in exchange for the final vatu they couldn't pay. I thought that was so cute I graciously declined which Alby complained bitterly about when I told him saying I should have taken the lollipop for him – oy vey!!!

Of course "Mr I can't stay still" kept disappearing from view. Over the coming days a chant regularly went up, "Where's Alby?" In fact when it hadn't happened for a while Andrew at one point pipped, "Well, no one's said it for five minutes… where's Alby?" By day three any one of

Jenny, Andrew and I could cue the others by saying, "One, two, three…" and then all three of us in unison would sing the familiar chorus, "Where IS Alby?" Tee hee.

On arrival in Tanna we were met by our guide, Peterson, and our main contact, Isaac, who saw us checked into our respective huts at Evergreen near the airport before taking a light lunch and heading off to the first stop, which, as I understood it, was the spring that would feed the water supply to villages we were aiming to help. The "road" (and I use the word only because there is no word in language that actually describes the condition) is something I will attempt to describe but truly if I showed you video footage of it you would still not fully be able to appreciate what the conditions were like unless you were there on it for yourself. The journey was undertaken in a truck with wooden benches and bars overhead to throw canvas over when it rained. When it wasn't raining we had the choice of either sitting on the wooden benches getting our bums bounced around or standing on the benches holding onto the bars, which was challenging to say the least but moderately more comfortable. All the natives travelled standing up, as did Alby, Andrew and myself, but Jenny sat throughout.

Now remember, Tanna is a volcanic island that appeared when an eruption threw the land mass out of the coral seabed. Consequently enormous chunks of jagged and razor sharp coral are embedded in the terrain of the land (and the "roads") as high as the island goes. The "road" to the volcano, which is a huge tourist attraction, is hair-raising, bone-jarring, and teeth-rattling enough, but please believe me when I tell you that the volcano "road" is like sealed tar compared to the "road" we took that first day (never, ever travelled by tourists) to the spring and the villages. This "road" was an almighty rollercoaster with hairpin bends, knife edge drops, coral encrusted edges, through thick jungle, and there was a risk we would have to return on it in the dark. As you stand being tossed around from pillar to post, and the vehicle lurches onto its side and swings back again, every so often someone would yell "low bridge" and we all had to duck or be garrotted by the undergrowth. There were times we became bogged, times cow dung splattered into the truck, and this journey took two hours passing by the freest free range cows, goats, chickens, and pigs that walk this earth – they would just skip out of the undergrowth in front of us as we were traversing another impossible bend, ditch, or incline.

We finally arrived at the home of "Louie the fisherman", the man who Ria (Alby's sister, hereinafter known as Maria) had innocently met on a footloose and fancy free holiday in Tanna as she was taking a snorkelling trip from his boat when she discovered this entire situation. It was Louie who lived nearby the villages that are in such dire need of a water supply, and he'd actually drawn out a map of what was where and what was needed that he gave to Maria, which is what started the whole adventure off. I was first off and marching onward when Peterson and Isaac told us, "The spring is this way" until I looked up… and up… and up. There was no way in my state of health/fitness I was going to be able to make that climb, even kitted out in all the right gear as I was. But that was okay, I was quite happy to remain with the truck and let the others go while I waited, after all I wasn't the one who needed to see how much water was there and assess the logistics – that was Alby's job, and when it comes to physical fitness and being able to do things normal mortals cannot, that is where Alby shines. And boy was he shining. It was so obvious he was so at home in this environment he was positively glowing.

There was no choice for the others – they had to go. Alby's role in all this was clear, Andrew had to take the pictures, and anyway Andrew is a strappingly healthy and fit forty-something who should have been able to take a climb like this relatively in his stride, and Jenny was the reporter, so she had to go as well. Jumping ahead, and I will backtrack to fill in the blanks in a moment, when they returned even Andrew said it was tough going, and Jenny, oh boy, her face was flushed beetroot and she was just about carried back down by two villagers. I think I made the right decision!!!!! Alby, it has to be said, just about skipped up and back with missing a heart beat – of course he did. To backtrack and fill in the blanks….

First of all no one but me was happy for me to stay literally in the middle of wild bushland unattended. I was really entirely relaxed about the whole thing but no one else was willing for me to remain alone so it was agreed that Isaac would remain with me… and boy did I get an education then!!!! Paul had told me before we left Vila about the "John Frum Cargo Cult" – a unique "religion" to Tanna Island. The story goes that during WWII great grey silver birds suddenly filled the skies above Tanna, the likes of which the primitive islanders had never seen before (these people were cannibals up until around 1950 – which could explain why there was some concern leaving me on my own!!). Anyway, these great grey silver birds dropped food and medicines from the sky – it was a miracle! And then the islanders saw something that really made their loin cloths stand on end – black men in uniforms giving white men instructions and the white men obeying them. You can imagine the impact that had. One of the black officers was "John from America" – hence where "John Frum" came from, and legend has it that he objected to the Christian missionaries coming to these islands and telling the people they couldn't drink their kava or sing their songs and that they had to wear Western clothes not straw skirts and bare breasts. What the (perhaps) well meaning Christian missionaries (some of whom were apparently delicious) didn't take into account was that in the tropics it rains – jungle rain – and if you're only wearing a grass skirt and bare breasts you get wet, then you get dry. If you're wearing Western clothes you get wet and stay wet and then get sick. John Frum told the people they had a rich and noble culture and they shouldn't give it up, and the people who follow his beliefs have become known as John Frummers. Isaac was one such person who ardently believed that John Frum was in fact their Messiah and where John sat on barren land fertile bushes would grow, etc and so forth. I was listening to all this quite goggle eyed when I suddenly heard cheering and chanting up ahead………….

It turned out that at the top of the climb the others had taken was one of the villages without a water supply and they were so delighted we had come to help them out they had staged a celebration. The group had been met with flower garlands, woven baskets, a feast in their honour, singing and dancing, and Alby had been invited to address the 200 strong audience. The spring was up there somewhere, but that was another TWO HOUR walk up a virtually vertical incline that even Alby said the group was not going to undertake – not because he couldn't have done it but because that would have meant two hours up and two hours back before they even got back to the village to start coming back down to me (another 45 minute damn hard climb) by which time it would have well and truly been dark and the return journey was not something Alby was prepared to let us undertake in the dark because he knew better than anyone (having done this sort of thing before) how utterly life-threatening that would be.

Saddened I'd missed out on the incredible celebrations, Alby later told me, "I just wanted you to be there – I'd have piggy-backed you up there if I'd have known"… how cute ☺ Jenny told me he spent half his time saying, "Oh Lynn would have loved this, I wish she was here" – isn't that nice?

While I was still with Isaac as the celebrations were taking place above us, Louie the fisherman's father appeared; a shrivelled old man with one remaining tooth and matchstick limbs whose eyes lit up when he saw I had cigarettes! Boy I could have bartered my way through Tanna with cigarettes if I'd have known – they were like gold to the natives. That might have been what was gold to them, but more golden to me was my 11th hour thought prior to leaving Australia to pack toilet paper and hand sanitiser – after all these long journeys, drinking, etc, and being in the middle of nowhere, well let's just say this turned out to be one of my better brain sparks!!! As for further details – just don't ask.

After the long climb and the gruelling ride home what did Alby do when we returned to Evergreen? He went for a run. Of course he did. Jeepers!

After dinner we all flaked out until I was awoken at 2.30am to the sound of scurrying in my hut. Of course there was no power in this place but knowing this in advance we had all brought torches along; which did nothing whatsoever to assist in discovering the source of the scurrying and once I was awake I was awake for the rest of the night. Even though I am routinely a very early riser, 2.30am was a bit brutal even for me.

The next day we were off to see one of the villages on the other side of the island where they did have a working water project, and the school where I was to gift my Magical Scarecrows goodies. After the previous day's journey these roads seemed like silk, but all things are relative. As we were being bounced around from pillar to post again I called out to Andrew on the other side of the truck… "And so when my mother asks if I was wearing a seat belt…" oh boy everyone belly laughed just as a particular jolt sent my hip flying into one of the bars! Oh crikey – PAIN!!! I didn't make much of it at the time, except to say "ouch" but when I looked later that night I had a bruise around the size of a male fist that was dark purple to black. It was later pointed out to me I was lucky I hadn't broken my hip! Never have I seen such a bruise. When I proudly showed off my war wound the following morning my travelling companions (Peterson, Jenny, Andrew and Alby) all gawped at it.

The village du jour was home to Pastor Japha (who had "married" Maria to her boyfriend Rob in a feather exchanging ceremony when they had stayed in this village). It was quite hilarious that everywhere we went Alby's single biggest claim to fame among the villagers was that (said in great excitement...) "This is Maria's brother!!" (When I later told Ria that she thought it was the funniest thing ever.) There was another obligatory flower welcoming ceremony, more gift baskets (each of the four of us were collecting baskets and flowers and feathers galore on every stop to the point where it was becoming quite ridiculous but there's no way we could refuse them or leave them – this was the villagers way of saying thank you, and being respectful, and showing they were not taking our kindness for granted – there would come a time when there would be a long discussion about Australian customs and immigration challenges, but for now they were just accepted graciously). Then it was cue the Magical Scarecrows........

Instead of going to the school from this village, apparently the jungle drums had sent out messages there was a fragile little white woman in the group who couldn't skip up and down coral encrusted muddy glades and glens like a mountain goat (or Alby) and so she was unlikely to have been able to reach the school and accordingly all the children were ushered down to us instead. About seventy children ranging in age from (I would guess) three to ten years gazed upon me with shiny, glowing, expectant, ebony eyes as I began my presentation by explaining what a scarecrow even was. You have to understand, where Port Vila is Third World, Tanna is about 66th World – we take for granted things these people don't even known exist. If you haven't been there you really can't truly appreciate how primitive things are. Back to the Scarecrows.......

They do speak and read Pigeon English in these parts, so I had brought with four of my most basic titles, not realising in doing so I had front covers respectively in bright red, bright blue, bright orange and bright aqua. I explained that my Scarecrows were magic, how, and why, and the stories behind the stories, etc. as the children listened in sheer fascination. Then I revealed my special surprise. I had also brought with me a stock of Magical Scarecrows harmonicas. Of course these kids had never seen a harmonica before, so I showed them how they worked. Oh wow that caused consternation. I asked for a volunteer to have a lesson and several put up their hands. Now the boxes these things come in are a bit tricky and stiff, so I told the kids we should ask Alby to open them for us, and when I looked around to see where he was he was already right behind me. The case was duly opened and he led the way in passing this wondrous device around for the children to try (and yes we have photos of ALL this). Each time one child made a noise with it all of them giggled – it was truly a moment of pure magic. I had also brought with a basic book on learning how to play the harmonica which I gave to the teacher and said when I returned I hoped to hear a chorus on harmonicas and then extracted my Blackberry to show them how it could really sound............

Before leaving Australia I had filmed some You Tubes of children playing "rock around the clock" and such like on the harmonica. Well, you can imagine if they hadn't seen a harmonica before they certainly hadn't seen a cell phone or moving pictures before – there were all sorts of "oos" and "ahs" as they clambered to get a look at this magical device and images coming from it – yes, we have photos of that too. Then Andrew suggested handing out the books, which Alby and I did to hungry little hands grabbing at the offerings. They went out so randomly that when Andrew asked the children to hold the books up it was a sea of colour. I couldn't have dreamed up a better shot. He put me in the middle of the children and when the photos are released, if I can get permission from the magazine, I want to make this shot the home page of my website. You just can't believe how wonderful it looked. Alby said it was a once in a lifetime shot. What an absolute triumph. I was quite literally jumping up and down with excitement.

Alby then went off and had a long one-on-one chat with Pastor Japha, after which (getta load of this!!!!!!) he came up to me and said, and I quote, "That's the Pastor who married Ria. Now he wants to marry me off." It took me no time whatsoever to reply, "Who to??!!" He just answered, "Well, I dunno." And then..........

Talk about being put on the spot! Alby was once again asked to say a few words. The day prior he'd had no choice but to do so, but this day I was there and he flatly refused to speak saying I should do it!!!!!!!! What the????????!!!!!!!!!!! Jenny said my expression changed from shock, to horror, to disbelief, and a few other emotions in the space of several seconds but apparently there was no wriggling out of it, and we were duly ushered into the "meeting hut" where the elders, the chief, the Pastor, Alby and Jenny sat waiting and looking to me to say something intelligent. Oh shit!!!!!!! I mumbled something about good things happening to good people and because this village had opened their hearts and their homes to Maria and Rob their situation had come to our attention and now our hearts were open to them and bla de bla de bla – it all went down very well. Alby said it was absolutely beautiful and the chief came up to us all afterwards and said he had been very gladdened to hear Mrs Lynn speak ☺ After which..........

We were ushered into the "refreshment tent". Oh boy! Again, there was no refusing, although when I returned to Vila and told Paul about this he pointed out I was the one person who could have actually refused (remember Paul's surname before the name change was "Bloomberg") by saying it wasn't kosher… but I really don't think that would have been politic – not to mention explaining "kosher" might have been moderately challenging. The four in our group sat cross legged on the bamboo floor eating I don't want to think what as the Pastor and Chief sat with us eating nothing, just watching us say, "Yum – lovely – thank you."

More tribal dancing – a farewell song – more gifts (how many baskets, grass skirts, fans and feathers was that now???) and it was back to the truck for more standing and ducking. You've seen my jungle hair from Africa – now transpose it to these conditions – talk about windswept and interesting!!!!

We had learned by this stage not to bother asking anyone in Tanna what time something would happen or how long something would take. Three different people would tell you three wildly different things, all of which were equally unreliable, as was trying to pick a midway point and taking that as a likely logical estimate. That's probably one of the reasons Alby is so at home in these places – that's basically his time keeping policy too.

The jungle rains started on the way to our next stop – the Sunrise huts close to Mt Yasur, the only accessible active volcano in the world. The canvas top was up and down over the truck as it rained – stopped – rained – stopped – and a new game began. Andrew's cap kept flying off. Peterson always offered to run after it but never one to miss an opportunity for a run, Alby was always first away to chase after it. I actually believe Andrew was enjoying this so much he might have let it slip a couple of times on purpose just to say, "There you go Alby – FETCH!!!" and off Alby would dutifully run and retrieve. Oh, by the way, I told you they spoke Pigeon English – at one point I was introduced by one islander to another as Alby's "Geographer"… well, I guess that isn't entirely inaccurate.

As we approached Sunrise we passed a car going the other way (a daunting enough prospect in its own right) but when I learned the car going in the opposite direction was carrying a woman in labour – the mind boggles!!!!!! Can you think of a worse place to be in labour than bumping around on those roads????

I had intended to have a shot at climbing this volcano but in the prevailing conditions decided it would simply be far too foolish, so Jenny and I remained, handing the boys our rain jackets (funny how the girls thought to bring them and the boys didn't - hum) and Andrew and Alby headed off with Peterson to see how Mt Yasur might perform that fateful night. Muscles I didn't know I had were all starting to hurt by this point, and add to that Sunrise had forgotten to buy in any form of alcohol – the only thing at all was two thirds of a bottle of wine I had brought with me from Evergreen – and that wasn't going to go far between all of us. Nonetheless, I agonisingly waited for the boys to return before partaking, hoping I'd be able to slip Peterson a few vatu to go and find some Tuskers (local) beer for us. That proved to be a good guess – a mere forty minute round trip on bumpy and blackened roads for poor Peterson – by which time the wine was well and truly expended – no Chanukah miracles there. Nevertheless, Peterson was well rewarded for his efforts and he stayed on to enjoy dinner and a night of absolutely hilarity with these crazy white folks. We all laughed so much it was fantastic, and I've truly not seen Alby laugh so much in the entire seven years I've known him.

The volcano had performed beautifully, even though according to Peterson it was a very quiet night as things can go. Andrew had asked Alby to go and sit calmly in a thoughtful and reflective position right on the edge, waiting for sparks to erupt so Andrew could capture an awesome shot. A normal mortal may have balked at such a request, but we're not talking about a normal mortal, we're talking about Alby Mangels – he complied and so did Mt Yasur – and oh my goodness gracious me you should only see this photo – it is truly to die for (no pun intended). And don't think Andrew didn't play the "Alby... FETCH" game up the top of an active volcano again – he did – and Alby went after it and retrieved it. Why can't I train him that well???

There was another Aussie tourist staying at Sunrise to do the volcano tour – a single man from the Gold Coast who instantly spotted and recognised Alby and proceeded to come out with an absolutely classic line: YOU KNOW YOU'RE ON A REAL ADVENTURE WHEN YOU LOOK UP AND ALBY MANGELS COMES OUT OF THE HUT NEXT DOOR. Tee hee ha ha ha ha ha lololololol... like "I'm a real man now 'coz I've done something Alby Mangels has done!" Too funny. He said this chance encounter totally made his trip.

No one could quite believe I was still firing having been awake since 2.30am, so they all decided to take bets on how long I would sleep that night. I did end up getting five hours – a marathon for me – but not all in one stretch, and in the middle of the night, in complete pitch black – my torch batteries started to give out – oh schwepps!!! Before they totally died I extricated some fresh lithium batteries from my camera and managed to feel and fumble my way to change them over to the torch completely blind, and that worked – phew.

The settings for both Sunrise and Evergreen were quite spectacular, right on the ocean fronts of opposite sides of the island. During some of our hair raising drives we caught glimpses of a range of ruggedly spectacular views but it was literally quite impossible to get photos of any of those due to the conditions.

Day three in Tanna and the first stop was to see the chief who needed the wheelchair. It turned out he'd lost a leg in an accident five years ago and was so grateful for our assistance (more flowers – baskets….). Peterson was actually his grandson, a fact we didn't learn until that morning. The whole family gathered for a photo, including a completely naked little boy of about three years. It's a wonderful shot.

Next it was onto the "clinic". Oh my goodness. You just can't begin to imagine the conditions and you would die if you saw what they used for an operating theatre – a sparse wooden slab with a less than clean looking sheet over it with instruments lying around in the open in rusting dishes – it is unfathomable that in this day and age anyone is forced to endure such conditions, but then when you realise that the main hospital in Port Vila is 160 million vatu in debt and running out of its own supplies of antibiotics etc it is less surprising that the people of Tanna get no help from the capital. If you get sick in Vanuatu you don't go to the hospital, you go to the airport. All the ex pats have Med Jet Medical Evac insurance – an essential for living on the island.

After that eye opening experience it was onto the lava beds of Mt Yasur for Andrew to have some more fun with Alby. "Alby – just run half way up that active volcano and pose for me". So he did. "Alby – just strip down to your shorts and go wading through this stream with this bow and arrow." So he did. It was all a dream come true for Andrew, and never one to miss an opportunity to play the "Alby – go fetch the hat boy" game, that happened again as well. Peterson was killing himself laughing but he (and the rest of us) had not seen anything yet…………..

Apparently Andrew has a little competition running with one of his mates to see which of them can get their photos taken naked in the most unusual or famous locations. You've guessed it. It just had to be done. He gave Alby his camera and went marching up to Mt Yasur, stripped down to his birthday suit (with his back to us) and leapt in the air for Alby to capture the shot… which he did… just as Mt Yasur belched and threw up a smoke plume as if to say, "Who dares mock me so?" (Talk about having smoke coming out of your ****!!!!) The shot was amazing, because seeing the smoke plume proves it was an active volcano as opposed to just some mountain, and best of all for Andrew he can label the photo as "Shot by Alby Mangels". Peterson laughed so hard I thought he might give birth to a lava rock… not that we all weren't doubled over in hysterics. It was incongruous to say the least that all this hilarity was taking place in the eerie and deserted landscape of one of Mother Nature's most awesome powers, belching and rumblings sounds in the background, ominous clouds rapidly rolling in, and a silly white man jumping up and down naked as a peeled banana in the middle of it all!!!!!!!!

It was quite incredible how "civilised" Evergreen seemed after returning from Sunrise – Port Vila will positively feel like the big smoke and I just can't fathom what it will be like to be back in Australia after all this. Andrew said he's going to have to hire a driver and stand up with his head through the sun roof!!! Seat belts??? Tar covered roads??? A power supply??? What are those things???

My trusty little high frequency mossie repellers really worked – I have returned without a single bite. The one time I did take the device off (for a shower) and forgot to put it straight back on there were six mossies around me instantly and the moment I reattached the device – pooffff – gone! Someone could make a FORTUNE selling these things in Vanuatu!!!!!!!!!!

Incredibly – my suitcase is trashed… my clothes are trashed… my hat – you don't even want to know about my hat… but I didn't break a single finger nail! Ha! Howzat? Jenny couldn't believe it! I was, however, quite sick on the last night in Tanna. About 1am I awoke with my entire body shaking. I thought at first I was just cold, and pulled on a pair of trousers and a jumper I had but that didn't come close to stopping the tremors. Then I realised I actually didn't feel too good – at all. My whole body seemed to be rebelling against something and for the life of me I couldn't get warm. I truly had visions of everyone taking me straight back to Australia and to hospital. I didn't know what was wrong with me, although I was quite certain it wasn't malaria because (a) it takes longer than that to present, (b) I didn't have a fever, and (c) I didn't have a single mossie bite. Nonetheless something was wrong. 1.30am I went hammering on Alby's hut door, "I don't feel so good!" He piled some more clothes on me to try and stop the shaking, which just wouldn't abate, before tucking me back under the covers (how cute) and all we could do was wait and see. I told him I'd be fine, but not long after he left I think the true cause presented itself – I began expelling from all orifices – not a pretty sight. I've been to the doctor today and we're pretty sure it was food poisoning of some sort. It's a little bizarre because all four of us ate exactly the same things for 48 hours and I'm the only who became sick, but who knows? Other than feeling totally beaten up the next morning I seemed to be fully recovered.

There were no arguments about window seats on the return flight from Tanna to Vila as the plane was just about empty so we had a row to ourselves each, which didn't stop Alby shouting down the plane to me, "Have you got a window seat?" Tee hee. All the baskets came back with us – we couldn't leave them because word would have got back. Then came the discussion as to what to do with them so aside from one I kept for myself Alby was tasked with taking them all through customs, thinking if anyone was going to get away with it – he would.

Paul met us all in Vila and took the group back to his pad to be regaled on tales of our adventures and a slide show from Andrew, while Jenny, Andrew and Alby waited out their transit time and I settled back into "MY" home (the bungalow in Paul's property). Truly as we drove into Paul's driveway I said, "It's good to be HOME" – and that is EXACTLY how I felt. Alby and I got straight into the pool – just for a refreshing swim but he couldn't help throwing in "And it's Mangels and Santer to the finish – and Mangels wins by an arm's length – then they go again – and it's Mangels pulling away…" like I could race him – bah humbug! I just snapped back, "Oh up your nose," hearing Jenny giggling away in the background. I guess that was payback for a snipe I got in at him over breakfast that morning for forgetting an envelope that had been meant for Jenny which he said that WE had forgotten (grrrrrrr). I explained to Andrew, "Now you see why I have high blood pressure!" Although truly, in hindsight and retrospect, my comment (which I won't repeat) was rather unkind and uncalled for – especially after he'd just cared for me being sick the night before. It's just a case of old habits die hard I guess – it's tough to break the pattern, although I must confess to seeing him in a totally different light and with new eyes since this trip. Kind of a shame we probably won't see each other again for many months or years the way our lives go in different directions, but such is life.

Paul laid on a wonderful lunch for everyone before driving them all back to the airport for their return flight to Australia (I was staying on for several days yet). There were hugs all around on departure. Everyone had enjoyed such a wonderful time, everything had gone so magnificently well, it exceeded all expectations, and Jenny and Andrew (both vets in their profession) said it was one of the best trips they'd ever been on in their lives. We all felt that way – it had been amazing. I put my arm around Paul and said, "Well, it's just you and me now," to which he quipped in reply, in front of everyone, "Yes, I thought they'd never leave!" LOLOLOL.

After we deposited the returning travellers Paul and I headed out to the Yacht Club for a drink when Paul admitted he liked Alby a whole lot more than he'd expected to. "He's smart – he's human – and I really like him," Paul smiled thoughtfully.

It was then back to Paul's pad, chilling out to the view, sunsets, martinis, balmy breezes, strains of Horowitz playing Rachmaninov from the speakers, and the sheer and true blessing of padded seats!!!!!!!!!! What a change of pace. The final cloud of that night's sunset was perfectly choreographed to the next musical refrain, Frank Sinatra singing "What are you doing for the rest of your life" – it literally brought tears to my eyes as I thought back over the past few days.

It was then off to the Anchor Inn for the Friday night ex Pat gathering to meet up with some friends, before heading out for dinner at the Casino. Talk about an international group: Paul – American; Outi – Finnish; Zvika – the Israeli who masquerades as an Italian; Bill – Chinese from the Caribbean; Ted – born in Egypt of Irish parents and educated in five countries; Tania – Kiwi; and me – the very uncalm Russian Romanian Gypsy Jew ☺

Still wearing my jungle hair I noticed a large bug buzzing around the patio the following morning, which inexplicably suddenly disappeared. A while later I went to push my hair behind my ears and – you've guessed it – I felt something scrunchy in it. Oo yuk – the bug had become tangled in my mass – still quite alive – and I had to carefully extricate it. That mission successfully accomplished it flittered through my mind what Australian customs and quarantine might have had to say about that if I hadn't spotted it! Honestly you could hide the crown jewels in my jungle hair LOL.

I have to say I am so pleased I took detailed notes of everything as it happened because if not for this record so much happened so fast I would have lost detail on one of the most wonderful memories of my life. Already it feels like it's slipping away like a dream. This has been the most magical time and I wouldn't have missed a moment of it for the world. Truly I am sad it is behind me.

Signing off…
Auntie Lynn ☺ xxxxxxxxx

The wheelchair I purchased for the chief

My windswept and interesting Tanna look

Paul Mason, Jenny Brown from New Idea, Alby and me

**All the children of Tanna receive a
Magical Scarecrows book**

**Lynn and Alby show the children how to play Auntie
Lynn's Magical Scarecrows harmonicas**

Return to Tanna (Dec/Jan 2010/11)

27th December, 2010, amidst the worst rains in Queensland in recent times, Darren Russell and I boarded an aircraft bound for what I now consider my island home of Vanuatu. Carrying over 80 kilograms of luggage, mostly medical supplies for the clinic and gifts for the villagers, the first pleasant surprise came when I presented my overweight invoice and credit card at the counter only to be told there would be no charge due to the nature of our mission.

The next challenge was going to be getting this lot through customs in Port Vila. Incredibly that all happened without a hitch too so my next question was, "How much damage occurred during the Boxing Day earthquake?" I was told there had been a few landslides in Tanna but there had been no structural damage or loss of life (I just wondered what this might mean for those horrendous jungle tracks we were going to have to traverse).

Due to the fight connections it was necessary to overnight in Port Vila where we had dinner with Noel Begley, one of the men who now runs interference for us with packages we ship over for the villages to ensure they clear customs in Vila and arrive at their intended destination in tact. Over dinner we heard some absolute horror stories of child-abuse that defied belief, the most shocking being of a couple who became so out of control on kava they boiled their own baby – and ate it! That was two years ago and the people involved were jailed for it, but so much for cannibalism having been wiped out 60 years ago.

Noel is married to a girl from Tanna (Liz-Beth) whose own sister (still living in a remote village on Tanna) regularly beat her three year old daughter who was born from a man she hated. The child had been so badly beaten an arm had been broken, there were welts across her back, and more. Noel and Liz-Beth have since taken the child off the mother and are raising her as their own but have not yet been able to make her smile or hear her laugh. Armed with many gifts for the villagers I rummaged through my bag of tricks and pulled out a jar of jelly beans, an inflatable beach ball and two of my most animated celebrity readings of my Magical Scarecrows stories – those read by the adorable Barry Crocker and ever effervescent Leo Sayer. I hope both men will be pleased and proud to know that I later learned when Liz-Beth sat down in her home in Vila (where they have a DVD player) with this young child who had never smiled and watched those DVDs – SHE SMILED!!! Well done guys – that's what makes the Magical Scarecrows so magical – people like you!!

The island of Tanna is also reputed to have some of the best coffee on earth. Being a bit of a coffee aficionado, Darren was very interested to try it. Hurriedly we finished our dinner and raced to the supermarket in Vila (which didn't close until 9pm) but arrived just too late. The next morning as we were boarding the plane in Vila to head off to Tanna (having collected ANOTHER 20 kilograms of luggage from Ria Snel – Alby's sister who runs the DAD charity – this was a case of clothes and toys she had FedExed over in advance for me to collect in Vila to take over with me for villagers in Tanna) Darren and I were literally handing over our boarding passes and about to step onto the plane when Noel came screaming through the airport calling, "Stop! I have coffee!" We looked at each other and grinned, stepped back, and waited while Noel ran back to his truck and collected not only a fresh pack of flavoursome Tanna coffee but a little pot in which Darren could brew his favourite beverage on the island without the use of electricity. Only in Vila!

We were met in Tanna by our trusted guide, and prince among men Peterson, the man who owns Sunrise Bungalows and has the only email on the island Isaac, and Louie the fisherman (who is the man who brought to Ria's attention the issue of villages without a water supply). The first business of the day was to hand over Ria's bag to Louie, and (given my surname and the time of year) I just could resist the "Santer" hat..........

I also received some updated information on the water project from Louie to pass on to Ria back in Australia with more detailed maps and technical specifications. As these papers were handed over, Peterson asked me, quite loudly, right in front of Darren, **"Does Alby know you're back here with another man?"** What the heck was THAT about? He knew I wasn't "with" Alby last time, and by the same token I wasn't "with" Darren this time!!! Still, I couldn't help chuckle and much as there was no need I dare say Alby would like to know that Peterson was watching out for "his interests" (too funny).

Isaac had not been well for a while so the next port of call was to stop off at his home (nearby the airport) and see what could be done. Darren may not be a medical doctor in Western understood terms, but he is an expert with herbal remedies and not a half bad diagnostician using ancient traditional methods and remedies that have been handed down through his ancestral family line for generations dating right back to his Druid ancestry. The device you can see him using in the photo here is a soft laser light he uses on acupuncture pressure points – with astonishing success!!

Peterson started absorbing Darren's information like a sponge almost from the word go, and while Darren was working on Isaac, Peterson made some hurried calls from his mobile phone only to come and inform me that we were going to make another pit stop before heading to the village of Pastor Japha as planned. Peterson wanted me to meet his sister who ran a little local radio station and she also wrote for the main Vanuatu newspaper. He felt what we were doing needed a wider audience and his sister was just the right person to spread the word.

With information duly exchanged between Lynn and Leslyne we were off to our first scheduled stop and our next drop off at Pastor Japha's village. Here I was gifting a big box of gifts for the children, including inflatable beach balls which turned out to be an ENORMOUS hit with kids in the village (of ALL ages) and a ton of beads and jewellery making equipment with which the women could make earrings, necklaces and bangles to sell to the tourists to make some money. It also gave me an opportunity to hand over the copy of New Idea magazine (that had come out 20th December) with the story about Alby's and my recent trip to assess the logistics of the water project for the villages. I have no doubt that the ever smiley Jenny Brown and Andrew Jacob (the reporter and photographer from the magazine) would be heart-warmed to see the photo of villagers checking out their story with absolute fascination.......

Of course we couldn't leave Pastor Japha's village without people coming forward with ailments they wanted treated as soon as we explained who Darren was and what he did. Naturally first cab off the rank was the chief, quickly followed by Pastor Japha himself.

Seeing the great success Darren was having with his treatments, Peterson asked if we could make another unscheduled pit stop at his brother-in-law's house as this man had been sick with headaches and unable to get out of bed for two months. Of course we agreed and when I checked in with Peterson the following day Darren's treatments had once again proved to have secured an improvement in the ailing man.

Back on the bone-jarring jungle tracks we passed three locals who wanted a lift. Peterson asked me if I minded if they hopped on board (which of course I didn't) and hence we picked up three big, black, machete wielding hitchhikers – but hey, any friend of Peterson's is a friend of mine… no problem………..

I had forgotten in the brief few weeks since my last visit how there was a drop-dead-stunningly breathtaking Hollywood view around every corner of the hairpin bends and cliff edge drops, but nonetheless this didn't make the going any easier than last time (in fact I think it might have been a little worse) and then…

We stumbled across another vehicle that had become bogged in the mud and mire. We had to help, firstly because we were going nowhere until the other vehicle had been moved, and secondly because how could we not help?

Of course no trip to Tanna would be complete without a trip to famed Mt Yasur volcano – the world's only accessible active volcano – and boy the old man ("old man" is the translation of Yasur) was really putting on a show – most likely due to having been disturbed by the recent earthquake. He was shooting fireworks and tossing out lava rocks like it was going out of fashion – sending many of the tourists up there running and screaming for their lives. Darren snapped some absolutely incredible photos that night (which I shall procure later) and on the journey back to Sunrise bungalows learned that Peterson had once travelled out of Vanuatu… to… TOKYO!!!! Talk about "from the sublime to the ridiculous"… you could not find a more relaxed people than those who live in Vanuatu, and, well, I don't need to explain to anyone the opposite end of the scale in Tokyo! "From Tanna to Tokyo" – it sounds like a song title, doesn't it? Apparently a film crew from Japan had been visiting and wanted Peterson to return with them to translate information from Bislama to English and hence put him up (all expenses paid) in a hotel in their capital city for two months. When I asked him what he thought of Tokyo he kind of sighed and shook his head. I understood!!!

As dawn crept over the horizon on a new day, I found a pretty little lizard curled up asleep in the clothes I'd laid out for my next adventure on Tanna. Seemed a shame to disturb him but it was probably time for him to move on too. This day was the moment I had been waiting for – when I was finally going to get to deliver all the medical supplies that had been requested from the clinic run by Nurse Nellie Shil. Nellie was actually on Vila at the time, visiting some relatives over the holidays, so we were met by her nursing aid, Kwaneamik, and members of the administrative committee, including a perfectly delightful fellow by the name of Joseph. Before I could hand everything over, which I was (you will understand) just ITCHING to do, the locals wanted to perform their pre-planned program for us, and honestly I couldn't have been more deeply moved…

After Darren and I were garlanded with flowers the entire congregated gathering stood to be led in prayer by Joseph who thanked the Lord Father Holy G-d for sending Lynn Santer to them to answer their prayers. Truly – I couldn't speak!!!!!!!!

Peterson translated as council members gave thanks but the nursing aid read from a prepared speech written in English. Then came the gifts – beautifully hand-woven mats that they sleep on and traditional feather wand-shaped sticks, which they asked me to touch as they blessed them. Along side these gifts they brought out three live chickens and I have to confess I swallowed my heart thinking, "If they sacrifice those things to me I am going to DIE on the spot!!!" Happily that didn't happen, they were just symbolic window dressing and I was able to breathe again.

FINALLY I was able to lay out all the goodies and go through the entire stash with the representatives on hand. They were totally blown away by the quantity, quality, and diversity of goods and medicines.......

There were whistles, and sighs, and general sounds of amazed gratitude as I explained everything. I DID RECEIVE ONE **HUGE** LAUGH from the locals when I reached the very large quantity of condoms and confessed I was rather glad that customs in Vila hadn't hauled me up and questioned me on that one as I might have had a very difficult time explaining they were all for personal use – LOLOLOLOLOLOLOLOL!!!!!!!!

Needless to say there was a LONG line of people waiting to see Darren as word had already begun to spread like wildlife around the island that a "doctor" was in town. They understood he wasn't a Western doctor as we understand doctor to be, but he was there and willing, ready and able to assist and the people flocked. Of course a huge issue is of basic hygiene, and in this respect Darren was able to explain the virtues of simple white vinegar, which is easily accessible, and as the days continued I don't think I have ever heard the word "vinegar" mentioned so frequently in rapid-fire Bislama conversations I could overhear everywhere. (Buy shares – stocks are about to go up!!!! Is that insider trading???)

Lynn touches the mats to be blessed

Joseph also told me that with two more visits to Tanna I can officially be accepted as "A woman of Tanna" and be given a custom name. Of course I wanted to know what custom name I might be given. Joseph and Peterson are still thinking about that one.

Our driver from both the last trip and this trip so far suddenly went Missing In Action (MIA). You might think that's a bad thing. Actually it turned out to be a very GOOD thing because Peterson secured another driver with a twin cabin and… padded seats, electric windows and AIR CONDITIONING! Where the HECK had he been hiding that??? I must say it made the rest of the travelling seem positively luxurious compared to what I had been through thus far on travels around Tanna (remember I did say "compared" to – the comfy car didn't improve the condition of the "roads"). Did I mention it had PADDED SEATS? Yahoo!!!

Lunch was at the STUNNING Port Resolution white sand beach, on bamboo dishes lined with palm leaves. It was all perfectly pleasant – quite delightful actually – until the next driver (with the padded seats) also went MIA. I began to wonder if I might be wearing the wrong anti-mosquito fragrance this trip? ☹ Still, if you had to be stuck somewhere it wasn't a bad place to be stuck...

There literally wasn't another soul around so Darren, Peterson and I just lounged on the beach swapping war stories wondering when – and if – and when our new driver would return, until Peterson decided he'd run off and find somewhere to fill up his mobile phone (don't ask me where one does that in the middle of the jungle, but apparently there are places dotted around believe it or not). That left me with THE ABSOLUTELY LAST PERSON ON THE ENTIRE PLANET I thought I would ever be stranded on a tropical island beach with (i.e. Darren) as pristine aqua waves crashed against the deserted shoreline. To say it was surreal would be an understatement.

The isolation didn't last long and soon both Peterson and the wayward missing driver returned and we were off to the village of the late Chief Missiwaren (Peterson's grandfather). This is the chief I purchased the wheelchair for. I wanted to visit his grave and pass on gifts for the members of his village. I put both flowers on his grave (as by the local custom) and a stone (as by my own Jewish custom – and explained that symbolism to Peterson, which he greatly appreciated and respected) and quietly told the chief how sorry I was that the wheelchair hadn't turned up in time and how proud he should be of his really quite remarkable grandson.

Returning to Sunrise bungalows I desperately needed a shower and a Tuskers (the local beer – yes this is the only place in the world where I have actually drunk beer). There was another patient waiting for Darren and Peterson (who had become quite the prodigy apprentice of Darren by this stage) watched on as the jungle rains set in again and I sat on the balcony of my raised bungalow to make notes on the days activities……just as……………THE WHOLE PLACE STARTED TO SHAKE!!!!!!!!!!!!!!!!!!!!!!!!!!!!!!!!!!!!

Now these raised bungalows are hardly the most sturdy of constructions and would rock – a little – just walking around in them. But I wasn't walking around – and no one else was in there. Oh yes, you've got it – it was an after shock from the earthquake. I put down my pad and pen (which tells you how serious it was) and just watched the whole place rocking from side to side around me wondering how long it was going to last and if it was going to get any worse. It didn't last long and it didn't get any worse, and, well, it gave me something to write home about (like I was short of material for that!!!). What do the bungalows look like? Here………….

The shower and toilet

The balcony I was sitting on when the after shock hit.

The bedroom

Over dinner that night everyone was a buzz asking, "Where were you when the earthquake struck?" and I taught Peterson to say "L'Chaim" when having a drink (a traditional Jewish toast meaning "to life") – it seemed appropriate. I must have been completely exhausted because I slept for a whole, beautiful, blissful, utterly luxurious seven hours that night (absolutely unheard of for me). In fact I was so out cold that at breakfast the next morning I discovered I had slept right through the next aftershock, which apparently happened at 10pm and I was out cold!!

Darren and I had planned to do some actual tourist activities the next day but as usual there was a stream of people wanting Darren's administrations. I even got in on the act. I'd noticed a small wound on Peterson's leg which he'd left totally unattended and flies were happily walking all over it. It was pretty obvious to me it wouldn't be long before what was a very minor injury could become fly blown and infected and become an extremely serious injury. Using the hotly demanded white vinegar we cleaned it and then treated it with simple MediPulve power (an antiseptic and drying agent) and covered it with a simple band aid – simple to us but no such things exist in the jungle. I realise it is quite beyond our ability to comprehend in the Western world that such basic things as band aids can quite literally save lives in a place like this, but that is the harsh reality of this beautiful but brutal land.

We were just about ready to head off when a woman came running down the road towards us screaming for "the doc" carrying a small child. The boy (Alec) was 18 months old and had a gaping open wound on his arm from boiling water he had scalded himself on FIVE DAYS EARLIER (in fact Christmas day). The wound had been left untreated since then!!! We piled them aboard the truck and raced back to the clinic where there now was a supply of everything we would need. There is no doubt in my mind this child would have died from the size of the wound and inevitable infection that would have set in, but this little boy was so brave it was incredible. Of course he cried when the arm was opened to inspect the wound, but to calm him down before treatment Darren pulled out a ball to play with him and he was running around on his little bare feet giggling his head off with delight, which relaxed him for treatment.

We had somehow picked up a Japanese tourist that morning. I later discovered that he'd heard what we were doing and wanted to witness it all first hand. Okay – fine – no problem. However when we arrived at the clinic even that little incident took a twist of fate. Unsurprisingly there were yet more patients for Darren to see, but there was also a steady stream of people with very minor cuts on their arms and legs wanting the assistance of my magical MediPulve and band aids. If I would have brought a truck load of this stuff it wouldn't have been enough. So Nurse Lynn was now swinging into action as well, and as this was going on the Japanese tourist (who didn't speak any English – well, not much) pulled down his sock and revealed a terrible gash on his own ankle that was beginning to fester. More MediPulve and Band Aids!!!!

Nurse Lynn in action with the MediPulve and Band Aids

Even the hitchhiking Japanese tourist gets in on the act!

With the latest round of administrations complete we were able to take in a tourist attraction en route back to the airport... the "black magic tour" (which was nothing whatsoever to do with black magic at all). The extremely well-organised walking tour dramatically re-enacted the cannibalistic past of these people and demonstrated some of the uses of plants as effective stretchers to carry wounded on and so forth. The "presenters" were so well camouflaged that Rambo would have been proud of them – they could quite literally disappear into the vegetation before your eyes and completely vanish. Of course this was a very useful technique when they were waiting in ambush for the next tasty white morsel to come along, something they very clearly demonstrated by appearing from nowhere, grabbing my leg and growling ferociously. Of course most normal people, especially women, scream when this happens. I don't need to tell anyone reading this I'm far from normal. Not only did I NOT scream – I GROWLED BACK!!! Peterson couldn't stop laughing!!! (Does this surprise anyone? I guess not.) He said he'd never seen anyone do that before and I was a brave woman (too funny!!!!)

Naturally they had to make Darren "Chief" – YAWN... it's a boy thing!!!!!!!!!

Now… on that… (the "let's turn white man into chief to amuse the tourists" thing) I have to skip ahead to tell you the single funniest story of the entire trip. Apologies to non-Jewish readers who might not immediately understand how truly hilarious this is…

On Port Vila I have a Jewish Israeli friend called Zvika (actually he's a friend of Paul Mason's, the Hollywood movie producer who has a holiday home on Port Vila, but now he's my friend too). Anyway, Zvika has been on this black magic tour and this guy is a really larger than life character who oozes charm and charisma and has a voice like Topol you could absolutely drown in. He also ain't short in supply of chutzpah either!!! So… they duly made Zvika chief when he was on the tour and asked him if he wanted to make a speech (which they didn't ask Darren for some reason). Zvika didn't know what to say… so he SAID KADDISH (a traditional Jewish prayer) IN HEBREW. They liked this so much that the villagers asked for more. So what did he do? He led them in a chorus of *Hevenu Shalom Aleichem* clapping his hands wildly (a very up beat traditional Jewish song). They couldn't get enough of it. He had to do it THREE TIMES!!!!! Oh I nearly cried laughing when he told me that story.

Back to Tanna airport and a much needed visit was required before boarding the flight to Vila. I tell you this why? Because the sign in the toilet rather amused me: PISPIS LONG TOWEL BOWL – NO PISPIS LONG FLOOR……………
Oh………kay!!! And you'll just love the boarding call: a chap opens the doors, claps his hands loudly, and shouts, "Come – come!" I am NOT joking!!!!

Finally we were back on Port Vila, after feeling a little like I'd just walked out of the Twilight Zone, and I was greeted with a stunning rainbow from my balcony overlooking Port Vila Harbour. It was impossible not to take this as a positive omen. That night we were meeting up with Nellie (who runs the clinic in Tanna) and Tony from DHL (who is going to look after all shipping from hereon) for dinner. Nellie very kindly gifted both Darren and I straw hats that she'd made and told me that many people before had promised they were going to provide aid but I was the FIRST one who had actually done it!!! There were tears in my eyes. After dinner Nellie came back to the hotel for Darren to actually work on a complaint of hers (which he did successfully) and to my astonishment afterwards asked me if I could take her back to the lobby as she didn't know how to use an elevator. Now just stop and think about that for a moment. Nellie has been trained by an Australian nursing teacher and she knows her nursing and midwifery skills well enough, but having been born and raised on Tanna something as basic to us as an elevator is a complete mystery to her. When I tell you that things we take for granted these people do not even know exists – I am not exaggerating.

The next day was New Year's Eve and most of the time was spent lazing on my beloved Hide Away Island, which I consider one of the true treasures of Vanuatu. Truly I didn't want to leave this island nation – not ever – and one day I will – I WILL – go back and live there. Preparations for New Year's Eve were enormous and happening everywhere you looked. For us the evening was going to be spent with Zvika and Outi and their friends at the Waterfront Bar and Grill.

As Zvika and I had been introduced by Paul Mason, Zvika had a plan to call Paul in Los Angeles at midnight. I said I thought that was a lovely idea but did he realise it would be 4am on New Year's Eve morning in LA? This was Zvika. Did he care? (That's a rhetorical question.) Come midnight I phoned mom and Zvika phoned Paul. Mom was delighted. Paul...............was not!!! Zvika told me Paul wanted to speak to me so we swapped phones (Zvika's never met or even spoken to my mom before, so what did he say, "SHANA TOVA" - a traditional Jewish greeting for a high Holy day – gee this guy's a character!!!). I took the phone from a very grumpy Paul who by that time had collected a whistle for obscene phone callers and was blowing it down the phone (too funny!!!!). Fireworks were exploding from one end of Vila to the other – it was like the whole of Vanuatu was alight – and this went on for thirty minutes with some truly spectacular displays and when it finished I think every vehicle horn on the island began to sound. All over Vila it was one giant party.

New Year's Day was spent at Iririki Island where we met Noel and Liz-Beth for lunch and INSPIRATION STRUCK.....................

Listening to everything that had happened in Tanna, Noel suggested we should produce a book of basic medical treatment that the islanders can provide for themselves using things that are to hand, such as honey, vinegar, etc., etc. Of course in the past everyone knew about these "custom medicines" only too well, but with the interference of missionaries (whatever their intentions might have been) the fact is that much of the traditional knowledge has been lost and new diseases they do not know how to treat have been introduced. Well, gee, write a book... now why didn't I think of that... do I even remember what I do for a living????!!!!! So it was duly agreed that Darren would provide content and illustrations, Noel would translate in Bislama, and I will have the book produced in time for my next trip mid year.

I am sending Darren back to work with the villagers in March, when he will gather as much info as possible on what is easily to hand that can be used, as well as treating and training the locals. He will bring that back to me and I will have the book produced by the time I return mid year to celebrate my 50th Birthday (Peterson nearly fell over when I told him I was turning 50 this year). I plan to spend the actual day with my sister and her family in Darwin, but before or after that I will return to Vila and Tanna to celebrate with my friends there (that date will be based on when Paul is next in town… if he's still speaking to me after New Year's that is LOL). It's a very simple and quick typesetting exercise to get Darren's info ready to be published in book form, so no drama for me time-wise.

Zvika and Outi invited us to their palatial edifice for dinner on our last night, and the final meal on day of departure was at my favourite restaurant, Tamanu, which gave me the opportunity to start planning the Vila part of my 50th birthday celebrations with the owners, Diane and Yianni (who remembered me well as having been there several times with Paul).

There are still pages more I could write – but I will spare you. For now it was a sad but very temporary farewell to my beloved Vanuatu as the sun set on this particular chapter.

EXTRACTS FROM LYNN'S AFRICAN DIARIES

Chronicle One – written to my parents

Africa, Ngala, is what heaven must be like. This is, without doubt, the dream of a lifetime come true. Now I have done it, now I have survived it all, I shall tell you the truth, and the whole truth, about this trip. If the pictures come out you simply won't believe your eyes!

I made contact with your man Brian on arrival in Johannesburg, who immediately arranged to take me to lunch. After a few words about Norgine politics Brian's mobile rang and he asked if I would mind if someone else joined us for lunch. The someone turned out to be Stephen Doherty, Brian's pension consultant and an ex-pat Pommie. Given Brian didn't have a clue what I did for a living (in fact when you asked him to meet me he thought I was coming from Australia) this was really quite amusing. Needless to say Stephen and I had a good deal to talk about. As it happens I still had part of the information with me which the Social Security Select Committee sent to me after I returned from the Cannes Film Festival. I had nearly finished it, and planned to complete it before I left Heathrow (which I did). Stephen was quite keen to get his hands on this and in return offered to loan me his binoculars for my safari, which I hadn't thought to bring.

My first pleasant surprise was, believe it or not, there are more dangerous creepy crawlies in Australia than there are in Southern Africa – and that's the truth!!!

Finally I was on my way to Ngala. A one-hour flight from Jo'burg to Skukuza Airport in the Kruger on a 20-seater, then a transfer via the "transit lounge" read: (park benches in the open) onto a 12-seater Cessna Caravan. The only way into Ngala is by plane and the flight took 20 minutes from Skukuza, of which I piloted for about 10 when the pilot learned I had had lessons on the same aircraft she had learned on, i.e. a Tomahawk. I did think she would keep a close eye on me, as I was half watching the landscape as well as the controls, but when I looked around at one point she was happily gazing out of the window with her arms folded! Still, in a plane that size you don't need to deviate by much to know you're moving off course. This was how I began my first time in Africa ever – piloting a 12-seater aircraft over the Kruger National Park, something I would never have dreamed would happen in my lifetime! What a start!

The smell here is distinctive – not at all bad but very distinctive. On arrival I have to admit I was fighting back tears because I just couldn't believe I was finally here. A few words on Ngala ... some say it is within the Kruger Park but actually it is on the Western boundary. Fifteen thousand hectares of privately owned land for the 20 chalets in the camp. Ngala is the Shangaan word for "lion" and the place is just in a class of its own. For the first 24 hours I was the only guest, which was absolutely wonderful. It was the first time in their history they only had one guest booked in and were very concerned how a single white woman from London might react to this fact...

Fifteen thousand hectares and EIGHTY staff at my disposal ... I was in heaven!

I determined to make the best of this as it was not likely ever to happen again. The staff complement is made up of rangers, trackers, guards, kitchen staff, medical staff, etc. They are a combination of Shangaan and white South Africans. As soon as you arrive you are assigned a tracker, a ranger and a guard. The tracker and ranger remain with you on all tracks/drives. The guard literally escorts you to and from your room as there are no fences around the camp (although the word "camp" definitely does NOT describe the luxury here). Any kind of animal can wander in at any time. As a matter of fact as soon as I arrived I was greeted with: "Would you mind signing the indemnity form immediately as there is a bull elephant outside your quarters and we don't know when you'll be able to get in"!! Ha! As it turned out the elephant paid quite a few visits to the camp and on more than one occasion people had to dispute ownership of land – which wasn't much of a dispute with a bull elephant ... he won and we waited!

He seemed to enjoy the water in our swimming pool which was quite amusing and made for some good pix. The staff called him "Justin" because he was "just in" camp every time they arrived. At least this time it was only an elephant, last year a crocodile took a fancy to the pool. The rangers had to keep catching him and taking him back to the dam but he stubbornly kept returning until eventually they took him to a dam 11 kilometres away. I decided I would not go swimming while I was here!!! Also last year a lioness came charging through the open lounge while guests were sitting around having tea. She was chasing a bug which happened to fly into camp so she chased in after it. I am told it woke everyone up!!!

By complete fluke I picked the best time of year to come here. Winter means it is dry, not too hot (in fact the mornings and evenings are positively cold) there are few insects (despite this I used copious amounts of insect repellent) and the grass is short, which makes viewing easier. The game drives are in OPEN jeeps and, as I said, I had my own private tracker and ranger. It was truly too good to be true. As a matter of fact when other guests started to arrive, as the staff could see how incredibly special this whole experience was for me, they moved me to their only "safari suite" which is set away from the others with its own lounge, swimming pool, etc. The opulence and appointments of the safari suite defy description. Sufficient to say I shot a whole roll of film just of the suite and the shower ... the shower is a LARGE twin-headed shower room surrounded by only see-through glass looking out over your own private section of the bush. It gave me chills. Now I HAVE to come back!! Even alone it was interesting never knowing what might appear outside. Given how expensive this place is for a regular chalet I shudder to think what the safari suite costs, but frankly my dear.... Anyway, that's next time, this time they just gave it to me because they liked me.

On the first evening's drive I saw baboon, buffalo, crocodile, civet cat, elephant, hippo, giraffe, scrub hare, hyena, impala, jackal, kudu, rhino, tree squirrel, warthog, wildebeest and zebra – not a bad first night I would say, and all very close. Half way through we stopped at a waterhole for a G&T and to watch the hippo come out to graze. At this moment, by the waterhole, it felt as though my whole life had been leading up to that moment. Indeed I believe it was. While we were watching the hippo we heard noises in the bush. Suddenly there were about a dozen elephant arriving to have a drink. Just wonderful.

Knowing there were more guests due to arrive I asked to do a deal – if the staff promised to keep Americans and children away from me, I'd promise not to try and touch the animals. We agreed.

I had dinner on the first night with some of the rangers and a few other staff. The rangers are deliberately walked into trouble as part of their training and so we exchanged war stories. I was quite surprised to find I could match them war story for war story with anecdotes of my encounter with the blue-ringed octopus, the dust storm of Melbourne, my 4-foot monitor lizard in Mauritius, the blue tongue in Portsea, the time you stood on a crocodile, your lizards in Ghana, **Rotorua,** and the golden orb spider Karen found in a web across our front door. They have golden orbs and funnel webs here too but their venom isn't deadly, as with the Aussie funnel web.

Please note: All the stories referred to in the above paragraph have been excluded from this book because otherwise I would have had to produce the next edition of 'War and Peace'!!!

I fell asleep to a chorus of lion and baboon and for the first time I can remember I didn't seem to dream. At 4 a.m. a few vervet monkeys went for a walk across my roof but I was already wide awake by then anyway.

Now if you think I've been silly so far, wandering off into the African bush with a couple of strange black men, you had better have a real stiff scotch before you read any further. These are the bits I saved for email when you couldn't shout back at me...

On day two we went tracking for lion. They were being very elusive as there was a two-day old cub in the pride. Eric, my ranger, Sam, my tracker and I tracked for four and half hours in the morning (they tracked 12 hours all together). At one point Eric and Sam saw tracks leading into a thick part of the bush and wanted to investigate. Here I was in the middle of totally wild African bush, in an open jeep, unarmed, knowing there were lion nearby, saying: "Sure, go find the lion" – 1 was on my own for about 15 minutes and didn't feel one bit concerned, I just hoped I'd be able to take the picture before I got eaten, which needless to say I did not (get eaten). While I was waiting Eric received a call on the CB from another ranger. I had to explain he couldn't come to the phone right now. And if you think that was stupid, wait for this...

We heard of a leopard sighting in an area we were not allowed to drive through, the only way in was on foot. They asked if I was "game" but I was already off. The rangers are, of course, armed and supposed to know what they're doing but anyway, to be perfectly honest, I just didn't care. As I said, if this was going to be the last thing I did I would go happy and know I didn't hold back. So off we went. Baboons were screaming at us from either side and we did find leopard tracks but alas no leopard.

I did know. I was totally and fully aware of, how potentially life threatening what I was doing was and I can assure you I did not feel even the slightest pang of fear or anxiety, just wonder and excitement. You might be wondering how good my tracker and ranger were – well how good would you call being able to spot a chameleon at night, in the bush, travelling at 20mph, with only a spotlight? I'd call that pretty damn good. The rangers say, and I have to believe them, that all animals, with the exception of elephant, will run away from man given the choice unless we are very slow and quiet. In the case of leopard they either run to lead another predator (us) away from their kill or their young or simply out of fear because they know man kills leopard. They will only attack if they are suddenly startled or cornered or, I guess, unless they are really, really hungry. We knew she wasn't hungry because she'd been spotted with a kill.

If you haven't passed out by now, I'll continue...

On the second day I was changing after the morning's viewing for lunch when I noticed a mother and two baby warthog happily grazing outside my room. I just sat and watched them for ages, partly because I was amazed and partly because I wasn't sure whether I should walk past them. I was soon assisted in this but discovered the warthog family are quite comfortable around Ngala guests.

Even after the evening drive we had still not found the pride of lions. Eric was now taking this personally and, as he's from the Shangaan tribe after which Ngala is named. He said if we didn't find them he was going to rename the camp "Elephant Lodge". We did see African wild cat, duiker (small antelope), genet (a small cat) mongoose, serval cat (which is very rare) and steenbok (another antelope).

On the third day I was awoken by baboon and hyena cries, quite close. There's no doubt about it. Kodak definitely invented this place (I took ten rolls of film).

You may recall the story my South African friend, John Mitchell-Adams, told me about the time he went on safari and saw a hippo try to save an impala from a crocodile? Well, that is not so uncommon. It seems the herbivores just gang up on the carnivores whenever they can – it's quite remarkable.

Finally, on the third morning, we found the pride. You'll believe me when I tell you I was taking pictures through tears. Two males, four females and four cubs within two-three feet of our jeep and just wandering around. The female with the two/three day old cubs stayed hidden but the others were so close I was simply awe-struck. I want to get married here, I want to die here and when I die I want my ashes scattered here – that's the best way I know how to describe what I felt. Straight after this we drove into a herd of 160 buffalo, which was moderately impressive to say the least. It was very nice of Stephen to lend me his binoculars but clearly he'd never been on a safari like this, they just weren't necessary.

From here we drove out a bit to stop for coffee in the bush among zebra, wildebeest, impala and warthog. Ahh, what can I say? I had assumed this was breakfast until we headed off again and turned into a clearing where a fully cooked CHAMPAGNE breakfast was laid on with tables, chairs, table cloths, etc. right in the middle of the bush. Do you begin to feel a hint of the complete magic yet? I'm sad to say I was out of film by the time we reached the breakfast spot as I'd taken a roll and half of the lions.

Evening three we went back to our pride – the other two Ngala prides moved North when the winter approached. This evening our pride was on the prowl for food. They say, and I am living proof that it's true, that while the carnivores are hunting they may smell something interesting in our jeeps but so long as we don't get out, or stand up showing them there are really bite size pieces inside, all they see is a big green steel animal they don't understand and mostly ignore. I was much calmer at this sighting, in fact it seemed perfectly normal for the entire pride to walk past us, within INCHES of the open jeep. If truth be told I felt a sense of calm I've never known before. This time I returned to the camp to find a buffalo 20 feet from my door and the elephant back in camp. Not only was the bull back but blocking my front door when the guard came to get me for dinner – lucky I was now in a suite with a back door!

If you don't believe me, if you think I imagined or exaggerated any of this, I don't blame you – 1 feel the same way – so I took names of witnesses and pictures whenever I was quick enough to think about it.

That wasn't the end of the bull for the evening either. Dinner was in the open but surrounded by a 15-foot high bamboo wall with a door size opening and gourmet bar b q inside. We dined to sounds of the bull destroying the camp's trees until the sounds seemed very close. One or two curious rangers, and me, got up to investigate. The bull was RIGHT THERE ... his tusks literally touching the opening having pushed the aperitif trolley out of the way to get there! He had never done this before. Suddenly everyone was up (about 12 guests by now). The rangers ushered all us green horns behind the bar fearing he was going to actually push down the wall and come in. He did not. He saw we were boring humans, not trees after all, and returned to destroying the camp while we returned to dinner ... one Italian lady nearly needed sedating!

Day four we were very lucky to come across African wild dog hunting. Even some rangers have never seen this creature, there are only a few hundred left. I returned to find baboon and impala by my balcony. Vervet monkey joined us for lunch, not that I ate much. I imagine it's like being in love – 1 could hardly eat, hardly sleep, and it felt wonderful. After lunch I found an extended family of about 20 baboon drinking from my swimming pool.

Night four we came across a breeding herd of elephant with babies smaller than I've ever seen before (three months) grazing. We were happily watching them when a report came in of a leopard sighting. We literally charged to the reported location but on arrival the ranger who reported the sighting had lost visual of her (an adolescent female). Well Eric wasn't having any of this. He drove through what seemed like solid walls of scrub and thorns (while I ducked to avoid getting scratched to pieces) to find her. Suddenly he stopped. "Look," he whispered. There she was, just sitting looking back at us. So beautiful. We watched for ages until other jeeps appeared and we left for a drink.

After pouring drinks and a few moments reflection Eric suddenly said: "SHHH." We froze. "Elephant," he said, "lots, at the water hole." Blowed if I could hear anything but I jumped in the jeep anyway, scotch in one hand, cigarette in the other, and off we went. Sure enough there were about 30 elephant, a croc, and a couple of bats at the sighting. Eric turned his CB off for about 10 minutes before telling the others and then was so pleased with himself he called in a confirmed sighting of kangaroo!!

On returning this final night I found a gift on my bed and a note which read: "Dear Lynn, It has been our honour to have you here at Ngala, Best Wishes, The Ngala Team." The staff at Ngala was thrilled to have someone there who really appreciated the animals. They get a lot of people who go to say "been there, done that", some who think they're Rambo, some who are frightened of everything, some who think it's a theme park and animals are there for demand viewing, or some who think, because you can get so close, that really they're tame. I was a rarity to them.

Day five. While driving through the bush Sam, who was sitting on the front of the jeep, started gibbering excitedly in Shangaan to Eric. Eric stopped. Sam jumped in the back. "What is it?" I asked. "CHEETAH," Eric replied, with a big toothy grin. Wow, what a way to finish. The cheetah was sitting in plain view in an open clearing watching the world go by, and what a noble creature she was.

I only received one scare, an insect bite on the arm just as I was leaving which turned two fingers numb for about ten minutes. Oh well.

I am going to DETEST going to LA after all this, all I can say is it had better be worth it.

They had a visitors' book in the Safari Suite. I signed it thus....

All my life I dreamed a dream,
which never would come true it seemed.
That one day I would be alone,
In Africa watching wild game roam.

I love my home, don't get me wrong,
But I've wanted this for just so long,
that finally I could wait no more,
I opened up that fateful door.

You see I feared so much in going,
Fears of only private knowing.
I feared the place would never be,
As heavenly as I dreamed it be.

But more what if it truly was,
All that I dreamed so deeply of?
Then how could life be great again?
Would I only feel great loss and pain?

Another fear deep down inside,
Was I knew I would lose all pride.
I would take risks to be with game
And this might be my final shame.

With conflicts running in my mind,
I took the plunge and went to find
Myself, my soul, so off I flew,
to live a wondrous dream come true.

I went alone and in the wild,
My spirit became one of a child.
The sights I saw defy belief,
I felt such blissful true relief.

I tracked a leopard - on foot - at night,
I felt just awe, no pang of fright.
I found a pride of lions so grand,
I wept for joy to share their land.

I was nearly trampled by great grey beasts,
As elephant devoured trees in feast.
I have found heaven, there is no doubt,
Of this I want to scream and shout.

The wonders I have lived to see,
will be a treasured memory.
My dream has come alive for me,
My soul and spirit now are free.

Chronicle Two

Flying in over the dry and harsh but remarkably beautiful Namibian landscape was a breathtaking moment, one full of expectation and excitement.

From the moment I set foot on African soil nothing else seemed to matter. I was finally going to see the work of the AfriCat Foundation, a cause I support from afar with only slide shows and newsletters to update me on progress. The first project on this property (before there ever was an AfriCat Foundation) started when Wayne Hanssen rebelled against his father's hunting and culling activities. Being a realist Wayne knew farmers did have a genuine grievance against big cats and so began a search to find more productive methods to control the predator problem of Namibian farmers.

I was expecting to find a sanctuary for rescued big cats. These cats are often caught by farmers in tiny box cages and sometimes left for weeks with little or no food and water. What I found was Okonjima, a luxurious tourist resort with ten little chalets where people from around the world come to marvel at the beauty of big cats at close quarters. I was expecting to find very basic accommodation organised for a supporter to come and see where their money was going. Instead I was greeted with a drink, a large and comfortable bedroom and hosts of friendly staff all completely dedicated to the AfriCat project.

Within thirty minutes I found myself sitting cross legged on the lawns of Okonjima while Lise Hanssen hand fed the first three cheetahs she saved: Chui, Caesar and Chinga. These three had been saved before the concept of the AfriCat Foundation had been born; at that time Wayne was still busy training leopard not to take livestock. Yes, leopard can be trained – and so can the farmers. More later.

Chui, Caesar and Chinga are as tame as house dogs and just as friendly. One was saved from a car accident, one from someone who thought it would be fun to keep a pet cheetah in a cage and one whose mother had been shot. Chui was eating his treats right in front of me when he realised there was a strange lady sitting next to his "mum", Lise. He stood up to his full height and looked me dead in the eye, his nose about an inch from mine as I was still cross-legged. I could feel his warm breath as an expressionless gaze met mine. "Don't worry," said Lise, "he's just checking you out."

Indeed he was and must have decided I posed no threat as a moment later he resumed eating.

The AfriCat Foundation now has 39 cheetah on 150 hectares. The objective will always be to release animals to the wild if it is possible, either to a game park in South Africa or in a safer area of Namibia, away from farmers. In some cases, however, this will never be possible. Such is the story of Tyke and Spike.

Tyke and Spike

These two cubs were found by the side of the road. Tyke was badly injured. Spike was taken to the sanctuary of AfriCat while Tyke was taken to the local vet. Spike fretted badly without her friend; she would call for him constantly and refuse food. When the vet called to advise Lise Tyke's leg could not be saved there was great confusion. Under normal circumstances Tyke would have been destroyed but in doing this Lise was certain Spike would surely die as well. They decided to try an amputation.

Today Tyke and Spike are two healthy, happy adult cheetahs who care for each other deeply. If they are out of sight of each other for a moment they are calling each other – their reunion is one of licks and nuzzling which warms the heart. Tyke runs very well on three legs and lives a fulfilled and happy life – one he would never have known without Lise Hanssen and the AfriCat Foundation.

While the story of Tyke and Spike is a heart warming one it does nothing to protect the species in the wild nor to stop farmers and poachers from killing these animals. This is a far bigger project. Most farmers have no idea that by shooting cheetah and leopard they are in fact compounding their problem. When the dominant male in an area is shot Mother Nature must replace him and Mother Nature has a habit of choosing the best. Furthermore Mother Nature is highly selective, she won't choose the best of two or three she will choose the best from 15 or 20. Hence every time a dominant male is disposed of the farmer finds he has 15 or 20 to take his place from nomadic males living on the fringes.

The World Society for the Protection of Animals has funded an education centre at AfriCat aimed at teaching the farmers and their children about the habits of the predators who take their livestock. These cats only want to live. When their habitat and their natural prey are taken away by man it is only natural they will look to the next source of food. Their environment needs to be maintained and the farmers need to look into new ways of protecting their livestock through movement of their herds and through more effective fencing which the Hanssens assist in providing.

All of this you will learn about in a visit to the luxurious Okonjima resort. You will see habituated cheetah jump on the front of your open jeep to come and eat their nightly meal while Lise strokes them and tells you the case history of each one by name. You will hear the low rumble of their purrs as they return the love and affection Lise devotes to these animals. You will realise beyond doubt that these beautiful creatures have a right to live as nature intended and that only through the dedication of organisations like AfriCat will they stand a chance of a future on our planet. Already cheetah have become extinct in many areas of the world where they once roamed free. If we do not take action we face the prospect of our children only reading about these magnificent animals in books.

I mentioned earlier about the leopard project at AfriCat. Leopard, unlike cheetah, cannot be tamed. They are, however, highly intelligent – they can be trained. At AfriCat, leopard are being trained not to hunt livestock. Impossible? Not at all. The project is an inspired piece of brilliance. Cattle have bells placed around their necks. Leopard are darted and have collars put on. At this point the laborious process begins. Staff watch and wait. When a leopard approaches a cow or calf the animal moves, the bell rings and the leopard will receive a painful electric shock. Amazingly quickly the leopard learns to associate the sound of the bell with pain and avoids it at all cost ... and a leopard has a long memory. Up to five years after the collars have been removed staff have tested leopard by putting a bell in a half eaten kill they know the leopard will return to. On moving the carcass and hearing the bell the leopard goes into orbit. Thank you Mr Pavlov. Of course it was Pavlov who discovered how animals could be conditioned this way in his experiments with dogs where he rang a dinner bell and then fed them, discovering after sufficient time had passed that dogs would salivate at the sound of the bell even if there was no food because they came to associated the sound of the bell with dinner. In the case of the Okonjima leopards it was the reverse effect, the sound of the bell told them "danger" but the same conditioning technique applied.

But one cannot become complacent. In order to monitor leopard population and activity tit bits are put out for leopards each evening. From the close quarters of a hide, visitors to Okonjima get a clear view of these incredible creatures as staff check who is around the property.

One such leopard is Tyson, the resident dominant male who escaped death by inches. Tyson was caught by the operator of a hunting lodge in a box trap. The idea is the courageous hunters from around the world who believe it is impressive to hang trophy heads in their homes while telling guests of their daring tales of near death in the bush get to shoot these hapless animals in the box trap. Brave and courageous, eh? Anyway, Tyson was so distraught by his captivity he struggled endlessly until he tore a hole in the side of his face on the trap, thus the trophy was ruined and Tyson was released. One very lucky leopard indeed.

The AfriCat project at Okonjima is a wondrous and wonderful place to visit. Cheetah and leopard are not the only big cats you will see there, there are also three resident lions. It was never the intention of AfriCat to get involved with lions but when Lise heard the story of Tessie and Tambo, a brother and sister kept in small cages and fed porridge and dog food, she could not refuse them. These young cubs had ribs which were painfully sticking out over thin skin. AfriCat took them in and nursed them. Today, together with Matata, another rescued lion, they live happy and healthy lives at AfriCat. They cannot be returned to the wild for they do not know how to be wild. In fact as they do not hunt for food their only exercise is to play with the staff of AfriCat. Have you ever seen a full grown lion play tug-of-war or fetch? You will at AfriCat. It's a scene straight out of a movie. If the staff are late for their playtime you will hear howls of annoyance from these lions all around the camp!

The enjoyment of a visit to Okonjima is beyond measure. Apart from the big cats, my personal passion as you may have noticed, you will enjoy sumptuous cuisine, startlingly clear skies, a visit to the hides in the evening where you may see any manner of wild animals and you will go on bushmen trails to learn the ways of the local people. Fascinating. Although Steven is from the Kavango tribe and not a bushmen he learned the bushmen skills as a child and honed them for visitors to Okonjima. I watched this man turn a plant into a rope before my eyes. The tour of the bushmen is definitely worth an hour on foot over dusty red sand to explore, although their courtship rituals leave something to be desired ... you will have to go to find out what I mean.

Finally I was getting ready to leave, happily drinking a cup of coffee with a peace and contentment I have rarely known when a caracal (lynx type cat) appeared in front of me and began to roll in the sand. A little surprised I politely said "good afternoon" only to learn this was Shingi. Can you believe Shingi had been a private pet ... of a woman who lived in a FLAT in a town? She had not been fed properly and suffered severe calcium deficiency when she was confiscated by authorities and taken to AfriCat. Now she roams free around the grounds of Okonjima. She is fed if she asks for food otherwise she does her own thing ... to the extent of surprising all the staff when one day they learned she was pregnant. When the big night came it was realised she could not give birth naturally as due to her calcium deficiency her pelvis was too small. An emergency Caesar was performed and now 11 month old Max joins Shingi in high jinx around the camp.

In one such high jinx episode, ten tourists were sitting around a table having dinner, not knowing anything about Shingi and Max, when Shingi smelled dinner, jumped onto the dining room table, stole somebody's steak, and ran off. The poor woman didn't know whether to scream or faint, so did neither and sat frozen to the spot with an expression of sheer terror on her face. When Lise only retorted with "bad cat" I couldn't help but belly laugh!

I would recommend and encourage anyone who has an interest in these magnificent animals to visit Okonjima. It's an experience you will not soon forget and by simply visiting you will be assisting the survival of Africa's big cats.

As a supporter of the Foundation I funded the building of two new holding camps at Okonjima. Away from the other tourists I was invited to visit the holding camps to witness the feeding of some new orphans which had just arrived. On the back of an open utility I sat with Carla, Lise's sister, and a bucket of meat while we drove through another camp with ten habituated cheetah who were not due to be fed that day. It is an interesting experience sitting in the back of an open ute with a bucket of meat being chased by ten hungry cheetah!!

After the orphans had been fed we drove back through the same camp. The ten cheetah now realised they weren't going to be fed and so flopped down on the dusty ground. One did put its paw up on the ute just to make sure there was no food left but Carla soon put him in his place. Our driver, Anthony, jumped out of the ute just to make sure everything was all right. "Oh," I said, "can I get out too?" "Sure," was the reply. This is something I thought I would never do, walk among ten habituated yet not tame cheetah while they merely observed me. I was able to get at eye level with them at just ten feet away to take pictures – closer than this and they did begin to hiss a bit.

There is no longer a shred of doubt in my mind, Africa is where I was born to be. I have never in any part of the world or at any time known such peace and happiness and fulfilment as the times I have spent in Africa. It is obvious

I am not alone in feeling this way. I was amazed at the number of people I met in Namibia from America, England and South Africa who visited once, went home, sold up and moved back for good. Perhaps it's something to do with time having no meaning there. I was asked how long I was staying. "Until Monday," I replied. "Oh, until Monday," they said, "that's great. What day is it today?" It's more than this of course. The land is beautiful, the people are happy and there's a big job to be done – one everyone at Okonjima and AfriCat believe in with every fibre of their being.

My next stop on this occasion was the Conservation Corporation lodge called Phinda in Zululand. By a complete coincidence three of the rescued cheetahs from AfriCat have been released into Phinda. Phinda is the largest game relocation program in South Africa. Once desert forest the land was consumed by farmers over many years. Now the Conservation Corporation have painstakingly turned it back into desert forest. One by one all the natural animals of this habitat are being reintroduced.

Phinda is luxury in the extreme – a bit too luxurious actually. When I got into bed the first night and found the sheets warm I turned off the electric blanket I discovered in disgust. Three in the morning I turned it back on again! Phinda's private lounge in Richard's Bay airport out-strips any first class lounge I've ever been in and on this occasion I had it all to myself. Excellent.

Unfortunately one down side of being in such a remote area is that the phone lines occasionally go down – and when they're down they're down for days. I have a mother. Need I say more? I knew I had to call to advise I had made the criss cross across Southern Africa safely but how? Another lodge was radioed to see if they could call out. They could not. Oh dear. It was not until late the next morning, in complete desperation, I thought of trying my mobile phone. There seemed to be a faint glimmer of a signal so I began a wander around to see if it would strengthen anywhere. A staff member spotted me. We are not supposed to wander far in daylight (and nowhere at night) without an armed guard as any manner of creatures from lion to herds of elephant can literally appear at any moment in these places. I was advised there was a particular spot in the middle of a nearby field where they have seen people successfully make calls from mobiles and they would escort me there. To my, and my mother's, complete amazement it worked! We weren't the only ones amazed either. A family of warthog who had been watching me with much fascination decided all humans must definitely be quite mad.

I tracked on foot, and found, rhino. I ate dinner under shooting stars. I followed an adolescent lioness on her first solo kill – she hadn't eaten in four days and here the animals are wild; i.e. we do not interfere. My ranger was very concerned if she didn't eat this night she would die. She was successful so we had champagne over dinner in her honour with the man in charge of the relocation program, Les.

Now Les, as you would expect, is a colourful character. The most amusing of his anecdotes was perhaps recapturing a herd of elephant which escaped from Phinda. It was only the second herd to be relocated, rather than culled, from Kruger. The first had escaped as well. Officials told Les he had 24 hours to get them back or they would be shot and relocation stopped/culling encouraged. With only enough M99 (tranquilliser) to knock out two (there were 26) elephants he replied with conviction that he would complete the task.

The matriarch of the herd had broken the perimeter fences at Phinda in 35 places then trumpeted for the herd to follow her. The entire herd followed her right into neighbouring villages. Two and a half thousand Zulu had gathered by late afternoon to watch what was going on. The elephant were getting very agitated by this stage attacking anything that smelled like human; ripping washing off lines and tearing it to shreds. Les called a vet in the nearest town and told him to high tail it to Phinda with all the M99 he could carry. In the meantime Les darted the matriarch.

Staff at Phinda were busy building a bigger, stronger electric fence to hold the herd should they be successful. At the 11th hour the vet came charging to the scene with sufficient stocks of M99 but by this time it was pitch black and they had no torches or spot lights. M99 will keep an elephant down for an hour, perhaps an hour and a half. In a massive effort of co-operation two lanterns were hung from each elephant. I'm not joking, you know!! If the lanterns moved the elephant was re-darted.

Then came the winches. They weren't strong enough for some of the larger elephants and upended in their efforts to move the matriarch. The winches had to be tied to trees while the Zulus were getting very excited. By daylight the operation was a success and the herd was returned safely to Phinda. Today the herd is 40 strong and very happy in their new 15,000 hectare environment.

Finally I saw the cheetah at Phinda roaming wild and free as nature had intended it to be. This was truly a magic moment. I understand farmers wanting to kill animals which destroy their livelihood but with education and patience and rehabilitation this can be stopped. What I cannot and will never in a millennia begin to understand is how or why people kill these beautiful and loving and precious animals for "fun".

Chronicle Three

I just have to share my experience in Africa with you. I realise many people do not share my passion for the Conservation Corporation and AfriCat projects and so won't read this. If you do choose to read it however, I hope you can share a little of the drama, the humour, the magic and the spectacle that is Africa. If I can show just one person how rewarding, although sometimes hair-raising, seeing these projects develop is I will feel I have achieved something.

The following notes were written up immediately after each event happened...

The Conservation Corporation continues to excel. My pilot, who was to take me from Johannesburg to Ngala, was waiting for me as I stepped off the SAA plane – literally. They have their own passport and immigration control, which in this instance was just for me. I was not on the ground in Johannesburg more than 30 minutes when we had taken off again, headed for Ngala. The flight was as smooth as silk; the butterflies in my stomach were merely from being overjoyed to be back in this wondrous and magical land.

The weather is perfect and Eric has once again been assigned as my ranger. It's like coming home to an old friend. Although I had been travelling for 24 hours door to door by the time I arrived at Ngala the adrenaline was working overtime. I had no interest in unpacking or changing. The dawn tracks were well underway and I couldn't wait to get right out there with the wildlife. The staff are still raising eyebrows at me as I write wondering when I'm going to fall over.

By the way, Mum and Dad, that spider we couldn't identify which I nearly walked into on several occasions in the Gold Coast is all over here in summer too. Eric tells me it's a variety of Golden Orb but assures me it's "not very" venomous. I'll take his word on that, I don't plan to put it to the test.

HUH ... SO MUCH FOR THAT...

RAIDERS!!! Remember that scene with the spiders? I kid you not, that scene has nothing on this....

Other than in controlled conditions I had never managed an up close and personal experience with a wild leopard before now. Eric spotted a young male leopard up a tree. We had a pretty good view from where we were but Eric said if we drove around to the other side of the tree we could see much better. This meant driving thru thick bush in our open jeep which didn't bother me a bit – done that many times before. Eric didn't warn me that on this occasion the bush was alive, and I do mean ALIVE with giant Golden Orb spiders. Derrick, my tracker, sat on the front of the jeep with a branch to brush them away as we drove thru but there were just too many. (Eric and Derrick – do you like that? I'm not making this up you know!!) So here we are: me, Eric and Derrick (two very obliging Shangaans) and an open jeep in the thick of a gazillion giant spiders. At one point Derrick decided to hop into the seat behind me and kinda hung over me so the spiders would fall on him first. I can't tell you how many fell in the jeep. Eric and Derrick were picking them up and chucking them out as fast as they were falling in while I was just trying to pretend it all wasn't happening. Spiders! Why did it have to be spiders??!!!

How big were these spiders? Well, in the communal webs they build they can catch birds!

Considering I spent half an hour killing an eyelash which fell off on my first trip to Africa....?!*?

Why was I telling you this? Oh, yes...

The end result of this trauma was the best leopard experience I've ever had. The young male performed beautifully. First up the tree, then climbing down, next posing in long grass. I have some stunning photos from all this – though none of the spiders as my eyes were shut for most of that part of the experience. At one point the leopard was just 7 or 8 feet from us, staring right into my eyes. Incredible.

On this same drive we came within a few metres of four lazy lionesses and were told to get lost by a nervous female elephant with two babies. The elephant and her babies had somehow become separated from the herd and were none too happy to see us. Normally the elephant at Ngala are very relaxed but a female with one adolescent one juvenile had every reason to be nervous. Yes, got pix of all that too.

Being somewhat of a veteran at this by now it comes as no surprise to have troops of baboon and vervet monkeys playing on my balcony as I write. Actually I think I'd be indignant if they weren't there. They are also trying very persistently to get into my shower which is sheer glass.

The obligatory vervet monkeys and a family of warthog joined us for lunch. Two of the young warthogs, undoubtedly the boys, engaged in mock battle while a third, undoubtedly the girl, joined mum in gentle grazing.

We tracked leopard into the night. On the way we saw hyena and 5 rhino, including two babies. One of the 12-month-old baby rhinos decided to charge our jeep. This was a first for Eric as rhino normally run the other way if we get too close. Obviously this baby had not been taught that lesson by its mum yet who, by all accounts, seemed to give him a good telling off for doing such a thing. The baby actually hit the jeep but neither the jeep nor the baby seemed to be hurt by the experience.

We saw all the big five game on one drive, which I've never done before. That is to say elephant, rhino, buffalo, lion and leopard. Eric also did his chameleon trick again, spotting the creature in pitch dark with nothing but a spot light while travelling at 40 mph. I really don't know how he does it. I wouldn't have seen it standing still in broad daylight.

Today it rained on and off. Not to worry, we donned the weather alls and headed off anyway. In one of the dry spells Eric and Derrick decided to follow some lion tracks on foot. They asked me if I wanted to wait in the jeep or come with them. Silly question. Well, just when I thought Africa couldn't get any better for me we came across a mobile pride about 10 metres away. Nine lions in total. I'm afraid I don't have photographic evidence of the experience but the memory of this moment has been burned into my mind for a lifetime. We spotted each other at about the same moment. I was totally awe-struck. No, not one iota afraid. It was wonderful. The lionesses growled a bit but not very seriously, nonetheless Eric insisted I stood behind him. What a fantastic experience this was. Sorry Mum. Actually ... no ... I'm not ... not one bit. Yes, this was the closest they have ever allowed a guest to get to wild predators on foot.

This is the benefit of tracking alone on private land (as opposed to a National Game Park) with a native ranger who gets to know you over time. Most visitors to Africa come here simply to say they've seen a kill. I don't understand this. My thrill and delight is to see these animals wild and free in their natural environment, to be at one with them the way it was supposed to be.

The pride and I just watched each other for some moments (during which time I'm sure I had a really dopey grin on my face) until Eric had us back off slowly to a respectable distance while Derrick went to get the jeep.

Well, Phinda is going to be interesting. We are certainly not going to be doing any tracking on foot. Four months ago a stupid cameraman from a German film crew got himself killed by an elephant because he didn't follow his ranger's instructions. The ranger had told the cameraman to stay in the jeep at all times, but this stupid cameraman wanted to film the elephant in a certain light and when the elephant didn't oblige (you won't believe this) he got out of the jeep and started throwing stones at her to make her turn around!!!! Well, she turned around ... and right royally pissed off, picked up the cameraman in her trunk, bashed him against a tree, broke his back, and killed him!!!! Now the lodge is on security alert because of the incident. It seems some people just can't get it through their heads that these lodges are not Disney theme parks, they are the real thing (see footnote story). You ignore advice at your peril. For some, it seems, that means paying the ultimate price. There was another guest death here too, in '93. A seventy-year-old woman who wanted to go back to her suite and change her shoes during dinner. You are told on arrival and there are signs to tell you DO NOT go anywhere at night without an armed guard. So who did she ask for permission to go to her room? A guard? Her ranger? No, her husband who told her sure everything would be fine. The comfort and extraordinary experiences The Conservation Corporation show you seem to lull some people into a false sense of security. Lion fodder.

Sadly the elephant who killed the cameraman has been killed. Why can't people realise these are wild animals and we are in their land? Anyway, the lodge is virtually empty, which suits me just fine. Mind you, when there are only six rooms it's never exactly going to be full.

What I really want to see here is the buffalo roaming free as they were still in quarantine last time I was here. As I think I have told you, Phinda is a massive (15,000 hectare) reclamation and relocation program, the largest in Southern Africa. This means all the animals in Phinda have been brought from somewhere else in Africa where they would likely have been culled. Phinda also has some of the relocated Namibian cheetah from AfriCat, which is wonderful. Ngala, on the other hand, is built on natural game land.

Phinda and all the ConsCorp lodges are also involved in massive community projects, putting money in and giving employment to the local people where all their lodges are located around Africa.

Walther has been assigned as my ranger again. He promises to take me to the buffalo tonight.

No problem in finding game in Phinda, cheetah are walking right into the compound!

I saw my buffalo. They were relaxed and happy and have all stayed together in one herd. I couldn't have been happier.

Okay, so we couldn't track on foot but after the buffalo sighting we stopped at a water hole for a G&T and to watch the sun set ... and ... as it turns out ... to watch a crash of rhino walk right by us, around 40-50 feet away on flat terrain. The rhino had decided it was time for a drink too. I just watched them calmly walk by us one by one in wide-eyed amazement. A couple of them stopped to give us a cursory glance but decided we weren't worth bothering with and kept walking. Yes, I have pix.

While we watched the rhino we heard a leopard call ... then an nyala (antelope) alarm call ... then a bush baby alarm call (of course I recognised all these sounds instantly ?!?!*!?). We were off, but we didn't find the leopard on this occasion.

I received the loveliest compliment from Walther tonight. He said so few guests can get the pleasure I so obviously do out of simply watching an inactive predator, appreciating him for the magnificent and free animal that he is. Most, says Walther, would take a snap, say "seen that" and ask to move on. So, he asked, would I like to go on an evening drive? I hadn't heard of such a thing before but it turned out a psychotic lioness and her family (and we do mean family as opposed to pride) had been spotted. After dinner, says Walther, we can try to see them. We cannot see them during the day because she hides in thick bush and the only way in is on foot – and at Phinda that's forbidden at the moment. Dinner, who needs dinner? I don't. Let's go. Well, Walther wanted dinner and we didn't want to offend chef so I played quickly with some food and off we went. Ten pm and truly the only people out with the animals.

Why do we call this lioness psychotic? She breaks all rules. She's not interested in becoming part of a pride. Only wants males to mate (well, what else are they good for? Just kidding, guys!!).

This lioness has been known to kill up to three animals in one hunt, which is utterly unheard of for lion. She won't make nice with anyone except her own offspring and those she teaches to be as psychotic as herself. She's a big beast too, even by lion standards. A daughter from an earlier litter had been kicked out last time I was at Phinda to fend for herself. This was the lioness I wrote about climbing a tree to search for prey, not at all typical lion behaviour. These lionesses' hunting tactics are far more like the opportunistic and nimble leopard than lion.

The matriarch lioness had kicked the daughter out (a) to learn to fend for herself and (b) because she decided it was time for another litter. Once she had her new litter, and the male had been dispensed with (why hunt for him, eh?) she brought the daughter back into the fold to baby sit. Incredible, but true. I saw the sub adult daughter here in July all alone and fending for herself. I saw her tonight back with mum and four new four-month-old cubs.

When we came across them at first we only saw the two lionesses and three cubs, all pretty happy with themselves. A very warm family scene it was too but we wanted to know where the fourth cub was. With very little searching we found the fourth cub attacking a freshly killed wildebeest on her own: "I'm gonna grow up to be a big fierce lion just like mom and I'll bite the leg off anyone who says different". This big attitude of matriarch mum is definitely spreading it's genes to her offspring. Woe betide any new dominant male who enters the territory and tries to dispose of her cubs to instil his own gene pool into the ranks. Normally a new dominant male would do this without a problem but I don't fancy his chances against these amazons. Brilliant stuff. Yes, I have pix.

On the way back I saw another spider. Only one, thankfully, but then it only needed to be one. This thing was building Buckingham web. "What's he planning to catch in that?" asks I. "Antelope?" Walther laughed so hard he nearly fell out of the jeep.

Once we cleared Phinda's airstrip of zebra, warthog and rhino this morning it was off to their beach at St Lucia in the co-pilot seat of a Cessna 206. On landing at Mbazwana (buzz-waarn) Walther met me to take me the rest of the way. The government officials who control entrance to the marine park were more than mildly curious about a white female travelling alone in this area but Walther and Prince (our Zulu tracker) managed to convince them it was okay.

We drove 10 kilometres down the beach, that is to say we drove on the sand at the edge of the Indian Ocean without another human in sight. What can I say? Sand dunes which reach the sky and grow palm trees. Warm aqua surf. Snorkelling which truly rivals the Barrier Reef. The ocean is absolutely teaming with life. Around the rock pools in every nook and cranny you look there is a new form of life. More species and colours of fish than I could count. Some of these swam right up to my mask. Swimming around in the rock pools you get the impression you are swimming through caves. Spectacular. Walther and Prince had to drag me out when the tide changed, I just didn't want to leave. I wish I still had my underwater camera.

Of course Walther and Prince were running around the rock pools barefoot. Me, I had my dive boots on the whole time. I think they must have steel-soled feet running over molluscs like that.

On the return from Phinda's airstrip we saw elephant. The same herd that was involved with the recent killing. Elephants are very family minded and have long memories. A bull was flapping his ears at us. This is not a good sign. Well, we humans did kill their matriarch so they have no reason to welcome us. We took an alternate route back to the compound.

Kids, who'd have 'em? Tonight we found a female cheetah with four 8-month-old cubs on the hunt. Mum spotted a nyala and quite clearly told the kids to stay put and watch how she does it while she goes and gets dinner. I understood what she said perfectly. Typical kids, they waited until mum was out of sight and got bored. One of the cubs led the others in their own attack on the nyala, undoubtedly thinking they could do anything mum could do. Of course they were wrong and spooked the nyala before mum got a chance to make her move. We followed this family for ages to see how things would turn out when the head ranger called everyone on the jeep radios telling us all to high tail it back to our respective lodges as there was a storm on the way. No kidding, we had seen the distant skies glowing with spectacular lightning for some time and knew it was moving this way but we kept on going for one more minute, one more minute, one more minute.

The tail end of the storm was still with us this morning but it was only light rain, certainly not enough to stop me from going on a game drive. It was well worth it too if only to be in the middle of the sand forest when the rains have stopped. The sounds of the sand forest at this moment are pure magic. The chime of the barbet birds, the song of the crickets, the rich freshness in the air – these are the sensations of heaven. What a far cry from the sounds of traffic and pollution I am about to return to.

Ever seen a pride of lion freaked out by a herd of elephant? We were tracking a pride today while in radio contact with another ranger who was tracking the herd of elephant. As the tracks pursued we realised we were coming closer and closer together until finally we were in visual range of each other. The eles (elephants) and the lions came within 40 metres of each other (Walther estimates even closer). The pride had three 12 month old cubs who were fascinated by the sound of eles eating. Mum was on alert. There was much breath holding in the vehicles. Finally the scene passed without incident as the wind was such that the eles didn't catch the scent of the lions. At least now I know how long I can hold my breath.

Caroline, my friend from ConsCorp HQ in Tanzania, arrived today. We wallowed in champagne while I filled her in on all the experiences you are reading about. She came on our dusk game drive with us. We hadn't seen each other for a year and I'm afraid didn't stop talking the whole time. I could clearly see Walther and Prince thinking "women!" During the course of conversation I discovered tracking on foot has been stopped at all ConsCorp lodges except for the most exceptional circumstances, i.e. only certain rangers are allowed to do it and then only with a repeat guest they know will behave properly/not panic in the bush. This makes my experience with the pride of lions in Ngala with Eric and Derrick even more special, if such a thing is possible.

Standing on my balcony the last day at Phinda, listening to the sounds of the bush, I couldn't help but be moved to tears by the sheer magnificence of it all.

Namibia. Fun and games at the airport on arrival. Some VIP was leaving Windhoek complete with a fleet of tinted black limos. We were allowed to disembark the plane and then locked out of the airport on the tarmac in burning sun until his jet had taken off.

Telecoms are as unreliable here as in other parts of bush Africa I've travelled. Here there is no problem with elephants tearing down phone lines or satellite phones which go out every time it rains, instead there are huge birds' nests in the lines which play havoc with transmissions.

AfriCat had organised for me to stay in Otjiwa, a 10,000 hectare game ranch 10 kilometres from their project. The transfer from the airport and accommodation arrangements all ran as smooth as silk. Otjiwa had already organised an evening drive and dinner for me before I arrived. It's a lovely place. Although the 10,000 hectares are natural game land the compound itself is manicured. There are peacocks and many other varieties of birds wandering around along with Sam, a tame eland (large antelope, as big as a small horse). The compound itself is fenced so there's no problem walking around at night. I must admit it did feel a little odd rocking up to some strange bloke in the middle of Namibia and saying: "Hi. I believe you are expecting me." Then again, I have complete faith in AfriCat to organise things.

Tristan, who runs Otjiwa, asked if when I return to Namibia I would be interested in going out with his nightly anti-poaching patrols. They've been losing a number of rhino here to poachers who sell to the Chinese market (bastards) so now they have armed guards patrolling the property. Sounds like a damned fine idea to me. Poor Mum, how are your nerves holding up at this point?

The anti-poaching project has been quite successful. Many poachers have been caught and sentenced to 12-14 years. The problem is they are released in less than 2 years because the authorities can't afford to keep them in. In Zambia, where rhino have been all but obliterated through poaching, they have a shoot to kill policy. Namibia is too young a country to introduce such radical measures – yet.

It's 4am here as I write. The power went out about 9pm last night and has been out ever since due to storm activity in the area. Just as well I thought to buy that big torch to take with when I was in Oz. Of course there is much excitement here that it has rained. Water is now flowing into the dam which is good for all life in the area. This also means the roads between Otjiwa and AfriCat are partly washed away. Hum, I only have two hours at AfriCat to take the pictures I need. It almost never rains here –

typical. Now I'm concerned I may not make it in time and the weather will be awful for the pictures if I do.

Clever critters. The termites here are planting mushrooms in their termite mounds. Because the rain washes their tunnels away they plant the mushrooms which grow to the size of footballs and act like umbrellas. Clever, eh?

For those who don't know I'm in Namibia to take some pictures of AfriCat cheetah for the back of my novel. As I am donating a percentage of whatever I may make from the novel to AfriCat we want a picture of me and the cheetah for publicity. I have to get to AfriCat and take the pictures in time to get back to Windhoek ... Johannesburg ... London and start real work again. It's going to be tight.

Peter Thomson finally arrived to take me to AfriCat. Now there's an interesting fellow. He worked in finance in Brussels, Dusseldorf, Zurich and so on until he was 40. Now he has an 18th century home in Walton on Thames (UK) but has spent the last 15 years roaming the globe helping out all sorts of wildlife projects. He's here with AfriCat for 2.5 months.

The sun came out for the pictures. We wandered into one of the cheetah encampments at AfriCat with Lise Hanssen, who together with her husband Wayne runs AfriCat. Lise called: "Here kitty kitty," and before long two cheetah dutifully appeared from the bush. They purred like house cats and licked me. Wow!! I spent over an hour just romping around with them, sitting by their side, even cuddling one of them!! It was the MOST unbelievable experience, in fact so much so that on the way I remembered I had had a bag when I walked in. Now I know not to turn your back on a predator, no matter how well you know them, and I know not to bend down in front of them. At best they consider this "play" and at worst they consider it "prey" – neither option is good! But these cats were my friends now, right? So I ambled back to where I'd casually tossed my bag, turned my back on them, and bent down to pick it up. In a heartbeat one was charging at me. I didn't even see it! Luckily Lise did and at the speed of light got in between us otherwise I might have been lunch! Just as well Lise knows these "kitties" pretty well!

The Namibian cheetah and leopard populations are under constant threat from farmers, poachers and other man made problems. Only through the work of organisations like AfriCat do these great spotted felines stand a chance of avoiding extinction.

Let me put our affluent Western lives into perspective for you. For the cost of a pair of Escada jeans in Namibia you can build a holding camp for orphaned cheetah. The cost of staying at Otjiwa is about what it costs to travel from Paddington to Reading by train. The lives of the people and wildlife in Namibia are dependent on the rains which are scarce. Despite all this I have not met a Namibian, black or white, who doesn't have a ready smile. They love their land and our proud of it. As you arrive at the airport to leave there is a huge sign saying: Thank you for visiting our beautiful country. I don't know, perhaps there's a message in there.

Peter had to drive me to the main road in a 4x4 to meet my driver who was to take me to Windhoek. As my driver, David, was in a regular sedan he'd never have made it down the flooded roads to AfriCat.

When I met David he turned off his music. "No," says I. "Leave it on." "But," complained David, "this is black music." I offered that this white person has Eastern European gypsy Jewish blood in her veins and the music which turns us on is not so far removed. "Ahh, ooo kay," replied David with a big approving grin.

During my transit time in Johannesburg I met Tjaart Kruger of Q Data who wanted to talk about putting a paper to the Finance Minister, whom he knows, on second tier funded pensions. I had met Tjaart in London when I was giving a talk on the pension scene using my predator/prey analogy. Tjaart wants to pitch a project which is both of social importance and commercially attractive. Q Data sell the Amarta product in South Africa. Amarta is the product of Sherwood, a major partner of Oracle UK in the pensions' admin systems scene. After we'd discussed business I had to ask him about his surname. You won't believe this. Tjaart's great grandfather, Tjaart Kruger senior, donated the original land which has since become the Kruger National Park. Life is strange, isn't it?

I can't tell you how many times I stopped on that long long walk to the plane headed for London. Leaving Africa, each time I leave Africa, it's the hardest thing I've ever had to do.

Charged by rhino, a leaping black mamba, a baby spitting cobra, a mobile lion pride not 30 feet away on foot, a spider scene that nightmares are made of and yes, I loved every second. Okay, except maybe the spiders. Seeing the animals I have in some way helped run free – to me, it doesn't get any better than this. Of course my hairdresser and manicurist are going to have a fit when they see me – gone native doesn't describe it. Africa: a lifetime of experiences in one day, an eternity of magic in every moment. As they say at ConsCorp, there is just one planet. Let the footprints you leave behind show you've walked in kindness to all living things.
    Lynn out of Africa

Footnote story: I could tell you a dozen incidents about people who have got themselves killed by game in Africa because they have been plain stupid but this one has to take the cake. A Japanese tourist was in Kruger where you drive in closed vehicles and do not get out – ever. He came across a pride of lions with their kill and was merrily videoing the event when he thought it would be fun to be in the picture as well. He got out of his vehicle, rested the video camera in running mode on the roof of his car and trotted round to the lions to stand behind them and wave at the camera. Well, he got the film footage of a lifetime. Shame he'll never get to see it.

Yes, there is more…
but it will have to wait for the
next volume.

Please check in at
www.lynnsanter.com
to see a list of all my other
titles… celebrity biographies,
thrillers, DVDs, and of course
The Magical Scarecrows
range!

www.ingramcontent.com/pod-product-compliance
Lightning Source LLC
Chambersburg PA
CBHW071418050326
40689CB00010B/1890